I1009970

LUNCH SPECI

Mussels, toma
chilli, chard
Sourdough
w/WINE

EAT LIKE A LONDONER
AN INSIDER'S GUIDE TO DINING OUT

TANIA BALLANTINE

PHOTOGRAPHS BY KIM LIGHTBODY

F

FRANCES LINCOLN LIMITED
PUBLISHERS

CONTENTS

HOW TO USE

The chapters in this book are organised by type of place, type of food and type of occasion. But you'll also find a list at the back so you can search by London area (as well as a list for veggie-friendly and last-minute options).

Note that the 'see also' boxes at the end of each chapter aren't comprehensive (so, for instance, the chapter on brunch doesn't include every single restaurant in the book that happens to serve an eggs benedict). This is deliberate. Instead, it's a handpicked selection of places that would genuinely have been good enough to go in that chapter, if they weren't already being listed elsewhere.

You'll also find details of 'branches' following each restaurant. Plus a restaurant's best 'siblings' (once again, it's deliberately not comprehensive). These siblings are other places opened by the same owners, where the menu and decor may be different, but you still can still expect a similarly good experience.

INTRODUCTION

London. It's an easy place to get lost in. All the tangled, twisted streets, all the perplexing little alleyways. It's no wonder we spend so much time staring at our smartphones, trying to figure out where the hell we are.

As for the capital's culinary map, that's even trickier to navigate. There are thousands of restaurants all squashed into the metropolis, covering every budget and more than 70 national cuisines (and this doesn't even include fusion joints). In 2014 alone, 148 new restaurants opened their doors – that's almost three per week. Yet after a whirlwind of hype, when every blogger and their best friend descend upon a place declaring it 'hot hot hot', many sadly end up as flashes in pans. But not all. There's a select group of truly memorable eating destinations in the capital: the kind frequented by clued-up locals; the kind that are either enduringly cool, dish up terrific food or have a spectacular setting. Sometimes, all three.

And here is the defining list. An insider's guide that sorts the great from the merely good. For everything from a quick pitstop to a blow-out date night. You need never feel lost again. So go on, eat like a local. Eat like a Londoner. And enjoy.

CULT CLASSICS

CULT CLASSICS

Londoners are a fickle bunch. Every week, there's a hot new restaurant that they simply have to try. During peak restaurant-launch season, between October and December, up to 30 restaurants of note can open every month. But more often than not, once the dust has settled and the hype has died down, these places lose their glossy appeal as people move on to the next shiny new opening. Cult restaurants, though, are different beasts. These remain firmly on the must-visit list, the culinary bucket list for the capital's residents. They are either enduringly cool spots – places that feel every bit as 'now' as the day they first started serving – or they are the trailblazers, restaurants that have managed to change the face of the city's dining scene. Tick them all off, one by one, and then annoy everyone you know by rubbing their faces in it.

✦ BALTHAZAR

When Keith McNally opened the first Balthazar in New York, he took the essence of a large Parisian brasserie and gave it a liberal splash of eau de Manhattan: polished interiors, well-drilled staff and high standards in the kitchen. This younger London outpost follows that recipe. When it opened in 2013, hype had reached an almost offputting high. Thankfully, it's now settled into being a grand, glorious restaurant with an electric atmosphere, charming (mostly French) staff and a smart menu of Paris-via-Manhattan cooking: shellfish, escargots, steak tartare, moules frites and gruyere mac 'n' cheese. Open all day, it's buzzy from breakfast to dinner and right through to midnight.

—

4-6 Russell Street, WC2B 5HZ.
020 3301 1155
www.balthazarlondon.com
Covent Garden tube.

✦ BEGGING BOWL

If you ever wanted proof of how much Peckham has changed since its Del Boy days, just take a look at Begging Bowl. This Thai restaurant on villagey Bellenden Road is not some humble neighbourhood café, but a proper destination with a Londonwide fan base. A large, contemporary restaurant, all bright colours and throbbing beats on the speakers, Begging Bowl uses fresh ingredients like pea aubergines and holy basil to create a menu of tapas-style Thai-with-a-twist sharing dishes. Whether it's a salad of starfruit, cape gooseberries, cashew nuts and mint, a tumble of smoky aubergine, coriander and shallot with a poached duck egg, or a Thai green curry made with rabbit meat, it's all terrific.

—

168 Bellenden Road, SE15 4BW.
020 7635 2627
www.thebeggingbowl.co.uk
Peckham Rye rail/Overground.

✦ BURGER & LOBSTER

It's hard to imagine a time before Burger & Lobster. The first branch in Mayfair opened quietly in the last few weeks of 2011, but before long it had taken London by storm. It quickly spawned several offshoots, each with a different look (invariably sexier than the excessively wood-panelled original) – and this Soho outpost is the best. It's a big site that screams 'good times!' with red leather banquettes, booths and a long cocktail bar. As always, the choices are simply burger, lobster, or lobster roll (all excellent) with a small salad and huge fries, for a flat price of £20 each. Without doubt, it's still the best-value lobster in town.

—

36-38 Dean Street, W1D 4PS.
020 7432 4800
www.burgerandlobster.com
Leicester Square tube.
BRANCHES: Bank EC2R 8AR; Farringdon EC1M 4AY; Fitzrovia W1W 7JE; Knightsbridge SW1X 7RJ; Mayfair W1J 7EF; Oxford Circus W1W 7JE; St Paul's EC4M 9BE.
SIBLINGS: Smack Deli, Mayfair W1K 5BN (p63).

✦ CHILTERN FIREHOUSE

It may be a celeb hangout, but this Marylebone hotspot defies expectation by having substance behind the glamour. Staff are genial and obliging, and prices, while high-ish, are not so steep that you'll need to sell a kidney. Best of all though, the food is excellent. Super-talented Portuguese chef Nuno Mendes imbues homely dishes with his ultra-creative wizardry, so you get to snack on crab doughnuts ahead of steak tartare with smoky 'Firehouse' sauce, followed by a stunning Angkor Wat-like meringue in a moat of frozen apple panna cotta. The A-list crowd is often hiding in the VIP bar, so forget about them and go on a sunny day, when the leafy walled courtyard makes an idyllic place to tuck into a luxurious breakfast or lunch.

—

1 Chiltern Street, W1U 7PA.
020 7073 7676
www.chilternfirehouse.com
Bond Street or Baker Street tube.

✦ DABBOUS

Dabbous, pronounced 'Dabbou' and named after its chef/patron, Ollie Dabbous, offers high-end dining with an edge. Proof that haute cuisine restaurants don't have to be formal or stuffy, the interiors are a study in stylised industrial chic, all metal and concrete. Likewise, the cooking (though firmly anchored in classic techniques) has solid creative flair as well as whimsical, playful touches. Just look to dishes such as raw scallop with eucalyptus or a dainty rabbit pie with a baby carrot poking out of the top. Put simply, every plate is an exquisite, teeny-tiny masterpiece. Service is polished yet warm, and there's a cracking bar downstairs called Oskar's (named after Dabbous's co-partner Oskar Kinberg) which serves stellar cocktails.

—

39 Whitfield Street, W1T 2SF.
020 7323 1544
www.dabbous.co.uk
Goodge Street tube.
SIBLINGS: Barnyard, Fitzrovia W1T 2LY (p35).

✦ DEAN STREET TOWNHOUSE

Part of the Soho House group, Dean Street Townhouse is the best kind of members' club: the kind that isn't, but feels like it should be. There are four key areas: the dining room bar, where media types can be found; the red leather booth seats, for buzzy lunches and dinners; the Parisian-style boudoir in the adjoining room, perfect for high

tea; and a small strip of street-side alfresco seating offering some of the best people-watching in London. Food is retro Brit with a splash of French (wild boar terrine, smoked haddock soufflé, or the signature 'mince and potatoes'), and is always dependable. Best of all, if you get too sloshed on cocktails to make it home, there are 39 bedrooms upstairs.

—

69-71 Dean Street, W1D 3SE.
020 7434 1775
www.deanstreettownhouse.com
Piccadilly Circus or Tottenham Court Road tube.

✦ GRAIN STORE

Gentrification can be a wonderful thing. Once, King's Cross was rife with drug dealers, prostitutes and derelict warehouses. Now, it's almost unrecognisably sophisticated, with this one-time grain store the jewel in its crown. A gentle take on industrial chic – pale exposed bricks, rough hewn woods, concrete floors – the interior is set off by an open kitchen, where the cooking draws inspiration from across the globe, with a single philosophy: vegetables go first. That's not to say that the seasonally shifting dishes are vegetarian (though plates such as mushroom croquettes with pine salt, or toasted cornbread brioche with burnt leeks and a slow-poached duck egg are excellent), but that you'll also find show-stealing vegetables equally billed in an outstanding meat or fish dish.

—

Granary Square, 1-3 Stable Street, N1C 4AB.
020 7324 4466
www.grainstore.com
King's Cross St Pancras tube/rail.
SIBLINGS: Bistrot Bruno Loubet, Clerkenwell EC1M 5RJ.

✦ HARWOOD ARMS

The Harwood Arms may have a bar, host a quiz, and sometimes get boisterous, but this is no run-of-the-mill boozer. It was the first London pub to receive a Michelin star: its cooking has its roots set firmly in the British countryside and includes plenty of in-season game. Crisp pressed rabbit shoulder with lovage, carrots and dandelion; Yorkshire grouse with chanterelles, blackberries and brown bread sauce; vanilla doughnuts with damson jam and cream – a typical meal here. Or sit at the bar, order a pint of ale, and gorge on the Harwood's much-copied venison scotch eggs, just because you can.

—

Walham Grove (junction with Farm Lane), SW6 1QP.
020 7386 1847
www.harwoodarms.com
Fulham Broadway tube.

✦ HUNAN

At first, this small Pimlico restaurant may not seem particularly special. The decor is 'neutral' – some say dull – yet the cooking is anything but. As you sit down, you'll be asked two simple questions: 'Is there anything you don't eat?' and 'How do you feel about spice?' Important only because there's no menu: you'll simply be sent morsel after morsel of regional Chinese specialities, increasing in size, until you're stuffed to bursting. It's an experience that doesn't come cheap, but you won't regret a sublime moment of it.

—

51 Pimlico Road, SW1W 8NE.
020 7730 5712
www.hunanlondon.com
Sloane Square tube.

✦ LYLE'S

Once upon a time, there were three Young Turks. A trio of chefs from London's top kitchens who quit their day jobs to form a collective and showcase their talents via a series of pop-up dinners. One by one, individual projects beckoned: one little Turk now runs Momofuku in Sydney, another little Turk launched Shoreditch's prized Clove Club, and this little Turk – James Lowe – opened Lyle's. At lunch you can order à la carte (also speedier), but this place is most fun at night when the no-choice set menu kicks in. Just book your table (anytime from 6pm) and you'll spend a couple of hours working your way through a series of modern British plates (braised baby onions, mutton and anchovy cream, baked sheep's cheese), each one as delicious as the last.

—

The Tea Building
56 Shoreditch High Street (entrance on Bethnal Green Road), E1 6JJ.
020 3011 5911
www.lyleslondon.com
Shoreditch High Street Overground.

✦ POLPO

It seems like only yesterday that this first Polpo opened. A sexy Venetian 'bacaro' (sort of an Italian tapas bar, but don't let the owners hear you call it that), it wowed with its good-looking staff (frighteningly hip Soho types), good-looking interiors (hand-beaten tin ceilings, stripped-back walls) and good-looking small plates (Italy, by way of Brooklyn). That was 2009. Fast-forward to today, and Polpo has gained siblings across town, yet has somehow managed to never feel like a chain. You don't really go for the food, though it's usually decent: the tiny 'bites' – cicheti – and pizzas are best, followed by vibrant salads and fish dishes. You go for a slice of a 'scene' that just never gets tired.

---

41 Beak Street, W1F 9SB.
020 7734 4479
www.polpo.co.uk
Oxford Circus or Piccadilly Circus tube.
BRANCHES: Covent Garden WC2E 7NA; Notting Hill W11 3QG; Smithfield EC1M 6DR; and Polpo at Ape & Bird, Covent Garden WC2H 8HJ.
SIBLINGS: Mishkin's, Covent Garden WC2B 5JS; Polpetto, Soho W1F 0PL; Spuntino, Soho W1D 7PW (p47).

✦ ROKA

Of all the high-end modern Japanese restaurants in town, Roka is the coolest. Perhaps it's the location – in the heart of Fitzrovia rather than Knightsbridge – or its open robata grill, the showpiece of the dining room, where jumping flames keep things lively. You're certainly more likely to find locals here than in its sister restaurant Zuma (or Nobu, p170), dominated as that is by Wags, oligarchs and Home Counties bankers. Feast not just on the excellent charred meats (lamb chops with Korean spices, say), but also on modish sushi (seared sashimi; soft shell crab rolls), and the ubiquitous black cod. Just be sure to put the bill on an expense account. Preferably not yours.

—

37 Charlotte Street, W1T 1RR.
020 7580 6464
www.rokarestaurant.com
Goodge Street or Tottenham Court Road tube.
BRANCHES: Aldwych WC2B 4HN; Canary Wharf E14 5FW.
SIBLINGS: Zuma, Knightsbridge SW7 1DL.

✦ THE SHED

A shed isn't just for storing garden tools, tinkering with strange inventions or hiding from your other half. Turns out, a shed is a great setting for a restaurant too. Actually this Notting Hill hangout isn't a real shed – it just looks like one from outside, with its white wooden panelling and pitched roof. Inside, the outdoorsy theme continues, not just with the decor (lots of wood, wall-mounted farm equipment) or staff appearance (plaid shirts, ruddy cheeks), but with a thoroughly modern British menu of 'country'

ingredients given fashionable twists. Choose from 'mouthfuls' (mushroom marmite with confit egg), 'slow cooking' (carrot hummus, venison cigars) and 'fast cooking' (veal carpaccio, lamb from the Sussex family farm).

——

122 Palace Gardens Terrace, W8 4RT.
020 7229 4024
www.theshed-restaurant.com
Notting Hill Gate tube.
SIBLINGS: Rabbit, Chelsea SW3 4UP.

✦ SOCIAL EATING HOUSE

Jason Atherton's restaurants are like a box of Quality Street: everyone has a favourite. For pricey haute cuisine, it's Mayfair's Pollen Street Social; for skyline views, City Social; for a buzzy setting, Berners Tavern (p143). But to really eat like a Londoner, the choice is always Social Eating House. Smart enough for a special occasion, yet never obscenely expensive, it mixes old-world glamour with effortless Soho cool. The humming upstairs cocktail bar Blind Pig is a destination in its own right, while the ground floor dining room is electric. Modern British dishes range from jars of ham hock with piccalilli to roast Cornish cod with candied celeriac and a poured-at-the-table Madeira sauce. They're playful yet masterful and all brilliant.

—

58-59 Poland Street, W1F 7NR.
020 7993 3251
www.socialeatinghouse.com
Oxford Circus or Tottenham Court Road tube.
SIBLINGS: Berners Tavern, Fitzrovia W1T 3LF (p143);
City Social, Moorgate EC2N 1HQ; Little Social,
Mayfair W1S 1NE; Pollen Street Social, Mayfair
W1S 1NQ.

✦ ST JOHN

Pioneer of 'nose-to-tail' eating and the granddaddy of the clattery, semi-industrial setting, St John is now firmly part of London's culinary history. Dishes change daily but you can always count on simple classics like bone marrow and toast, British comfort food (grilled sardines, rabbit stew) and first-class puds (boozy prunes and choc trifle, bread pudding with butterscotch sauce). Given its meaty menu and clinical interiors, it's more appealing to alpha males; for a more feminine vibe, head east to Rochelle Canteen, ably co-run by Margot Henderson, wife of St John co-founder Fergus Henderson. In the grounds of a former school, 'ingredient-led' dishes such as polenta fritters or hare pie are served in a small café: it's loveliest in summer, when the outside seats overlook the grassy playground.

—

26 St John Street, EC1M 4AY.
020 7251 0848
www.stjohngroup.uk.com
Barbican tube or Farringdon tube/rail.
SIBLINGS: St John Bread & Wine, Spitalfields E1 6LZ; St John Bakery, Bermondsey SE1 2HQ.

SEE ALSO:
- Barrafina, p162
- Bocca di Lupo, p36
- Bull & Last, p116
- Ember Yard, p165
- Hakkasan, p99
- Hawksmoor, p156
- Koya, p60
- La Bodega Negra, p144
- Meatliquor, p157
- Ottolenghi, p180
- Palomar, p45
- Patty & Bun, p158
- Pitt Cue Co, p160
- Pizza East, p93
- Pizza Pilgrims, p94
- Spuntino, p47
- Towpath, p140
- Violet Cakes, p180

SMALL & BUZZY

SMALL & BUZZY

Small *is* beautiful, especially when it comes to London restaurants. It might seem counterintuitive that in a city so big, so sprawling and so densely populated, that the smallest restaurants can be the best. But here's the thing: small restaurants are often independently owned by people with a real passion for great food and great hospitality. Plus, they're pretty much guaranteed to be buzzy; put two people in a room that only holds 20, and you're already 10 per cent full. That sense of intimacy means these places are great for a heart-to-heart with an old friend, a low-key date, or somewhere you can eat on your own. Patiently wait for a table to come free and you'll soon realise size isn't everything.

✦ 10 GREEK STREET

With a nameless front, the ultimate indicator that this is a place for those in the know, 10 Greek Street quietly uses its address as an identifier. It makes it easy for cabbies to find while simultaneously creating a subtle sense of cool. Then again, 10 Greek Street doesn't really need the classic 'no-name' approach to be trendy: after all, it's a cramped dining room with wooden chairs, scrawled blackboard menu, an open kitchen and tap water served in milk bottles. And the modish, daily-changing Med-leaning food is all faultless – from mussels and clams with Spanish blood sausage, sherry and samphire, via poussin with bulgur wheat, parsley and chilli, to espresso terrine with chocolate walnuts.

—

10 Greek Street, W1D 4DH.
020 7734 4677
www.10greekstreet.com
Tottenham Court Road tube.
SIBLINGS: 8 Hoxton Square, Hoxton N1 6NU.

✦ BARNYARD

Who knew that hay barns and hoedowns could be so thigh-slappingly fashionable? Ollie Dabbous and co-partner Oskar Kinberg, that's who. The pair behind cutting-edge Fitzrovia fine-diner Dabbous (p17) are also the brains behind this casual and extremely affordable Charlotte Street joint. It may be themed to within an inch of its life, with distressed woods, oil-barrel seats and cheery staff in plaid shirts, but boy can the kitchen cook. Small plates of US- and Brit-inspired comfort food are elevated to well above their roots, from just-baked cornbread to outstanding homemade popcorn ice cream served with warm smoked fudge sauce. Yee-haw.

—

18 Charlotte Street, W1T 2LZ.
020 7580 3842
www.barnyard-london.com
Goodge Street or Tottenham Court Road tube.
SIBLINGS: Dabbous, Fitzrovia W1T 2SF (p17).

✦ BOCCA DI LUPO

Don't be put off when your bilingual friends tell you to go into the 'mouth of the wolf' (bocca di lupo) – it's Italian for good luck. Though you won't need luck as you enter this glamorous backstreet Soho restaurant. The first thing you'll come across is a glossy counter bar – this is where the theatre is. But if you're happy to forego being served across the bar, and you want seats not stools, the rear dining area is no less glitzy, with marble floors and closely packed tables. The sharing menu roams Italy's regions, offering dishes in small or large portions, all organised into sections such as 'raw and cured' (blood and pistachio sausage with pickled girolles) or 'roast and grilled' (suckling pig; breaded clams). Look out for a handful of dishes marked BDL: these are signature creations and guaranteed to please.

----

12 Archer Street, W1D 7BB.
020 7734 2223
www.boccadilupo.com
Piccadilly Circus tube.
SIBLINGS: Gelupo, Soho W1D 7AU (p182).

✦ CASSE-CROÛTE

You used to have to go to South Kensington for an authentic slice of ooh-la-la. No more. Now you can wander down Bermondsey Street – already home to many excellent independent eateries (including José, p43) – to this preposterously charming little bistro. There are only around 25 seats in a small room that couldn't look more the part. Monochrome floor tiles? *Oui*. Red-and-white-checked tablecloths? *Mais, bien sûr*. Vintage prints and pictures? *Naturellement*. The daily-changing menu deals in charcuterie and classics: fish soup, steak tartare, lemon tart, plus lesser-seen options, like calf brains or quenelles (creamy poached meat or fish 'dumplings'). And while staff may seem aloof at first, they'll become charm personified if you make the effort. How very French.

—

109 Bermondsey Street, SE1 3XB.
020 7407 2140
www.cassecroute.co.uk
London Bridge tube/rail.

✦ CEVICHE

Whether you sit up at the counter watching the super-friendly staff, or at a table in the just-as-buzzy back room, you are guaranteed a fun time at the near-faultless Ceviche. The Peruvian food is superb, and although you should focus on the eponymous citrus-cured fish (the signature Don Ceviche, a dish of lime-and-chilli-cured raw seabass chunks, is outstanding), there are also excellent anticucho skewers from the grill. Look to the octopus and chorizo or chilli-marinated chicken, and don't pass on the interesting salads (white quinoa with butter beans, coriander and avocado). Portions are small and intended for sharing, though you may end up fighting with your forks.

———

17 Frith Street, W1D 4RG.
020 7292 2040
www.cevicheuk.com
Leicester Square tube.
BRANCHES: Old Street EC1V 9NU.
SIBLINGS: Andina, Shoreditch E2 7DJ.

✦ DUCKSOUP

You can always guarantee a vibrant, friendly ambiance at this cute Soho spot, and the food is spot-on too. The daily-changing hand-scrawled menu is mostly infused with the flavours of the Med, from the South of France through to Italy, Spain and North Africa – that means deep-fried collard greens laced with chilli, chargrilled quail with cassoulet and girolles, and cold sliced lamb with pickled beans and labneh. Another passion of Ducksoup's is natural wines: these are chalked straight up on to a board and are changed as often as the food. The room may be tiny (most of the seating is along a single counter) but it backs up that old cliché: good things come in small packages.

—

41 Dean Street, W1D 4PY.
020 7287 4599
www.ducksoupsoho.co.uk
Tottenham Court Road or Leicester Square tube.
SIBLINGS: Rawduck, Hackney E8 3NJ.

✦ HONEY & CO

If you were just walking past, you'd never guess that this sweet little Fitzrovia café serves some of London's best Levant-influenced cooking (with ingredients from Turkey to North Africa, via Israel and Lebanon). The menu changes constantly, but the mezze are always outstanding, as are the slow-cooked meats. With its light space and pretty patterned floor tiles, the tiny room works best at lunchtime, or even for Saturday brunch, when you could tuck into a merguez sausage, harissa and egg bap, or one of the outstanding just-baked savoury and sweet pastries from the counter, such as Honey & Co's take on the Chelsea bun, made with sour cherries and pistachios. Just watch the bill, which is distinctly more restaurant than café.

25a Warren Street, W1T 5LZ.
020 7388 6175
www.honeyandco.co.uk
Great Portland Street or Warren Street tube.

✦ JOSÉ

There are plenty of great places to eat on Bermondsey Street, but the two offering the best combination of food, ambiance and price are bijou bistro Casse-Croûte (p38) and this equally tiny tapas bar created by Brindisa co-founder José Pizarro. In true Spanish style, it's a perch-at-the-counter space which has a nasty habit of getting ridiculously busy. But if you don't mind a bit of chaos, you'll be rewarded with superb small plates from the blackboard menus: ham croquetas, prawns with chilli and garlic, lamb cutlets with romesco sauce. For the same quality of cooking, but a more slick, civilised setting, try big brother Pizarro, just down the road at number 194.

---

104 Bermondsey Street, SE1 3UB.
020 7403 4902
www.josepizarro.com
Borough tube or London Bridge tube/rail.
SIBLINGS: Pizarro, Bermondsey SE1 3TA;
José Pizarro, Liverpool Street EC2M 2QS.

✦ MORITO

Semi-pedestrianised Exmouth Market, with its pretty strung-up lights and clutch of eateries, is always an atmospheric spot. There are plenty of good dining options, including handsome Medcalf and high-profile Moro. For guaranteed buzz, go for Moro's little sister, Morito. True, it isn't super-comfy (it only offers wooden stools, all backless), and the garish orange counters are a bit like eating on a giant Smartie, but for terrific small plates, brilliant service and real ambiance, it can't be beaten. The daily-changing menu presents tapas-with-a-twist: there are flavours from North Africa and the Middle East, too. Creamy, salty croquetas, vibrant dips (sweet, garlicky crushed beetroot with walnuts and feta) and salads (crispy chickpeas with pumpkin, coriander and tahini-laced yoghurt) are all divine.

—

32 Exmouth Market, EC1R 4QE.
020 7278 7007
www.morito.co.uk
Angel tube or Farringdon tube/rail.
SIBLINGS: Moro, Clerkenwell EC1R 4QE.

◆ PALOMAR

If you don't like rubbing shoulders with strangers, perhaps give the counter at Palomar a miss. Of all the sit-at-the-bar options in town, it's the most cramped, with the added 'charm' of a stream of people jostling past behind you. Still, it's great fun, plus you get to watch the menu of 'modern Jerusalem food' being prepped. It offers a modish take on the flavours of the Levant, the area around the eastern Med including Turkey, Lebanon and Egypt; the creamy polenta with shaved asparagus and a mushroom ragout and shakshukit (basically a deconstructed minced lamb kebab) is a particular must. But Palomar is as much about buzz as it is cooking, so rather than opt for the comfort and calm of the tables at the back, make sure you book a front-row seat.

———

34 Rupert Street, W1D 6DN.
020 7439 8777
www.thepalomar.co.uk
Leicester Square or Piccadilly Circus.

✦ SMOKING GOAT

Just when you thought we'd run out of new hipster concepts, along comes this Thai barbecue joint. Smoking Goat takes unstoppably popular dude food – chicken wings, lamb ribs, duck legs, plus the odd whole crab – douses it with punchy Siamese flavours (the head chef trained at cult favourite Begging Bowl, p13), and grills it over chestnut embers. The result is a huge hit with Soho creatives. There are typically only three starters, followed by three mains, which, for £15-£20, include dipping sauce, steamed rice and green papaya salad. The lean, bar-like room, with its dark green hues, scuffed-up wood tables and flickering candles, is always moody and atmospheric: it's the perfect place to lose yourself in a large bottle of sharing beer, or finish your night at if you're already three sheets to the wind... It certainly beats the hell out of a dodgy kebab.

—

7 Denmark Street, WC2H 8LZ.
No phone
www.smokinggoatsoho.com
Tottenham Court Road tube.

✦ SPUNTINO

Spuntino is kind of place your dad would hate – unless your dad is Mick Jagger, of course. It's hard to find (look out for '61' above the door); you can't book, but may well have to queue; seating is on backless barstools along a counter; music is grungy and loud; and the wine is served in tumblers. From the same crew as Polpo (p23), Spuntino deals in Italian-American sharing dishes, from sliders and shoestring fries to 'plates' (cuttlefish with gremolata and butterbeans, truffled egg toast) and salads (pickled pear with gorgonzola and walnut), dished up by friendly tattooed staff against a dimly lit backdrop of cracked, battered tiles and scuffed floorboards. Embrace your inner rebel.

—

61 Rupert Street, W1D 7PW.
No phone
www.spuntino.co.uk
Piccadilly Circus tube.
SIBLINGS: Mishkin's, Covent Garden WC2B
5JS; Polpetto, Soho W1F 0PL; Polpo (Covent
Garden WC2E 7NA; Notting Hill W11 3QG;
Smithfield EC1M 6DR; and Polpo at Ape &
Bird, Covent Garden WC2H 8HJ).

✦ WRIGHT BROTHERS

Although there are newer branches (including one at Kingly Court off Carnaby Street, which has excellent alfresco seating), Wright Brothers' cramped Borough Market original still wins the most hearts. Truth is, there's a certain magic to this oyster and porter house, with barrels in the window, battered wooden tables and fans idling on the ceiling. It's hectic, sure, and you'll probably have to share a table with strangers, but very few places in London have this level of rustic charm. The regularly updated blackboard menu advertises the foods of love – oysters, platters of fruits des mers, chocolate truffles – but if you're here just with friends, then check out the likes of devilled whitebait and haddock fish pie too.

----

11 Stoney Street, SE1 9AD.
020 7403 9554
www.thewrightbrothers.co.uk
London Bridge tube/rail.
BRANCHES: Kensington SW7 3DY; Spitalfields E1 6EA; Soho W1B 5PW.

SEE ALSO:

- Barrafina, p162
- Copita, p164
- Flat Iron, p155
- Patty & Bun, p158
- Pitt Cue Co, p160
- Polpo, p23

PERFECT PITSTOPS

MARKETS

PERFECT PITSTOPS

Rush rush rush. Sometimes, that's what London life is about. But just because you've only got an hour (if you're lucky) before you have to be back at your desk, or you're en route to somewhere else, it doesn't mean you should compromise on what you eat. There's a time and a place for that congealed slice of pizza by the tube station, and that time is never. Here's a handpicked list of the best places to go when you need a quick bite, as well as London's best markets for grab-and-perch meals from the finest food trucks and stalls. The selection is so good that if you do get the chance to linger, you should definitely make a meal of it.

✦ BABAJI

Londoners know that for traditional Turkish, you head to the stretch of Green Lanes in Harringay home to fabled restaurants such as Antepliler and Gökyüzü. But if you're in town and craving the flavours of Istanbul, then make a beeline for Babaji (Turkish for 'father'). Almost uncomfortably close to the clamour of Piccadilly Circus, the location is touristy, yet this is no trap. Created by veteran restaurateur Alan Yau (of Hakkasan, p99, and Princi, p62), it takes street food from his wife's native Turkey and serves it up with trademark flair. There are mezze and grills, but centre stage is the wood-fired 'pide'. Often called Turkish pizza, it's really cheesy flatbread, with toppings such as spicy beef sausage over chewy, salty sheep's cheese. The vibrant setting effortlessly combines Ottoman tradition with Soho chic: handmade tiles and bolster cushions in cobalt blue, uniforms of billowy Turkish trousers; designer chairs, clean lines, young staff. Babaji really is the daddy.

----

53 Shaftesbury Avenue, W1D 6LB.
020 3327 3888
www.babaji.com.tr
Leicester Square tube.

✦ BONE DADDIES

Move over, Tokyo; out of the way, NYC: you've no longer got all the hip noodle bars. This self-styled 'rock 'n' roll ramen bar' was one of the first to kickstart our capital's own noodle-bar trend and remains one of the liveliest, with its grungy Japanese posters and pumped-up music. Sit up at a high table (most are communal) and order a classic bowl of Tonkotsu pork ramen, or else try a house creation (such as the chicken broth-based T22, complete with 'cock scratchings'). Optional snacks like the amazing soft-shell crab with green ginger chilli sauce are great and may ramp up the bill unnecessarily, but are so good you'll be glad you couldn't resist.

—

30-31 Peter Street, W1F 0AR.
020 7287 8581
www.bonedaddiesramen.com
Piccadilly Circus tube.
BRANCHES: Kensington (in Whole Foods Market) W8 5SE.
SIBLINGS: Flesh & Buns, Covent Garden WC2H 9LX (p90).

✦ DOSA N CHUTNY

The lights are bright. The wipe-clean tables are functional. Ambiance, you could say, is lacking. But the dosas are so, so good. Made of fine-ground rice and lentils, then cooked on a large open skillet, these crisp-edged savoury crepes come either plain or filled (for instance with a warmly spiced potato stuffing, spiked with mustard seeds and curry leaves). All varieties – they make more than 20 – arrive with spiced vegetarian dips, chutneys and gravies. This is South Indian fast food at its best, and makes for a seriously delicious pitstop. If you really want to make a feast of it, the curries, breads and street snacks are all excellent too.

—

68 Tooting High Street, SW17 0RN.
020 8767 9200
www.dosanchutny.co.uk
Tooting Broadway tube.

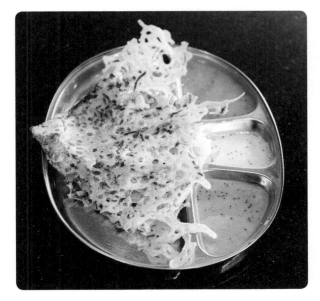

✦ HERMAN ZE GERMAN

In spite of the tongue-in-cheek name, this Soho sausage joint deserves to be taken seriously. Wursts are imported from Deutschland's Black Forest, where they've been loving made by a butcher called Fritz. Yes, really. Order at the counter and choose classic bratwurst (a fat, plain sausage which combines pork and veal), bockwurst (smoked pork) or chilli beef wurst (beef, pork and chilli). They come in buns with sides including sauerkraut, fries and potato salad, and with traditional sauces like sweet mustard and 'curry sauce' – a spiced ketchup, hugely popular in Germany. Unlike its other more fast-foody branches, this one has a fair bit of seating in a dark, sexy space of distressed wood and panel-beaten metal. You could certainly do a lot wurst.

----

33 Old Compton Street, W1D 5JU.
020 7734 0431
www.hermanzegerman.co.uk
Leicester Square or Piccadilly Circus tube.
BRANCHES: Charing Cross WC2N 6NE;
Fitzrovia W1T 1RS.

✦ KOYA

For many, udon is religion. When properly made, these thick wheat noodles draw worshippers from far and wide. Koya is no exception. The udon at this minimalist noodle bar are foot-pulled — yes, stretched by a clean foot — rather than machine-made, and the bounciest in town. You can eat them hot (in a hot broth) or cold (for dipping in hot broth), or cold with cold sauces for dipping or pouring. If you're more 'team ramen' than 'team udon', check out Tonkotsu (p64) or Shoryu (p137), and if shared tables aren't your thing, head to the long counter at the spin-off Koya Bar next door.

—

49 Frith Street, W1D 4SG.
020 7434 4463
www.koya.co.uk
Tottenham Court Road tube.
SIBLINGS: Koya Bar, Soho W1D 4SQ.

KOYA

Opening Hours
Monday - Sunday

✦ PRINCI

If someone told you that Princi was a self-service 'cafeteria', you'd probably get the wrong impression. So let's stick to its sexier-sounding Italian definition: 'una tavola calda'. Everything at this London outpost of the artisanal Milanese bakery is available either to takeaway or eat-in, though it's always busy, so go off-peak if you'd like to sit; the room is so supremely sophisticated you won't want to leave. The focus is on swish pastas, fragrant pizzas fresh from the wood-fired oven and sandwiches on just-baked loaves, plus antipasti, Italian puds, Continental pastries and even luxury doughnuts. All against a backdrop of sandstone and black marble, with a stylish uplit water feature around the edge of the room. Cafeteria? Hardly.

—

135 Wardour Street, W1F 0UT.
020 7478 8888
www.princi.co.uk
Leicester Square or Tottenham Court Road tube.

✦ SMACK DELI

This fast-food joint is from the folks behind the more obviously named Burger & Lobster (p14). The main event here is the selection of great-value lobster rolls – go for the Japanese-leaning Seven Samurai or the Thai-inspired Happy Ending, they're both terrific. Sides include rich lobster chowder, more like chunky bisque, and moreish courgette fries. Seating is mostly downstairs, where they've made the lack of windows a virtue by giving the place an edgy, nightclub-meets-minimalist-modern-dungeon vibe. Note the mystical-looking mermaids projected on to the walls, their hair swaying just enough to make you think you might, in fact, have been slipped something mind-altering.

26-28 Binney Street, W1K 5BN.
No phone
www.smackdeli.com
Bond Street tube.
SIBLINGS: Burger & Lobster (Bank EC2R 8AR; Farringdon EC1M 4AY, Fitzrovia W1W 7JE; Knightsbridge SW1X 7RJ; Mayfair W1J 7EF; Oxford Circus W1W 7JE; St Paul's EC4M 9BE).

✦ TONKOTSU

It's pretty tough to choose between the original two Tonkotsu sites (there's also a 14-seat ramen counter in Selfridges, so you can shop-slurp-shop). Tonkotsu Soho is tiny and edgy (rock music, concrete floors, rusty wire mesh on the ceiling), while Tonkotsu East is larger with a vaulted brick ceiling, bustling open kitchen and peaceful alfresco seating in bamboo-fringed area out front. It's certainly the more relaxed, convivial option. What they all share is top-drawer Tonkotsu ramen: a soup base with a deep, intense flavour and almost creamy richness, wholesome, firm wheat noodles, fresh (not tinned) bamboo shoots and half a soy-tinged soft-boiled egg. Plus a handful of small plates, for the truly greedy.

Arch 334, 1a Dunston Street, E8 4EB.
020 7254 2478
www.tonkotsu.co.uk
Haggerston Overground.
BRANCHES: Marble Arch (Selfridges) W1A 1AB; Hackney Central E8 1HR; Soho W1D 4QG.

MARKETS

✦ BOROUGH MARKET & MALTBY STREET MARKET

The street food stalls at Borough are more mainstream than you'd find at Broadway (p72), Brixton (p71) or KERB (p68) markets, but it's worth visiting at least once for a sense of its unique atmosphere and excellent eateries. Tip: go for toasted cheese sarnies at Kappacasein. Then it's time to break free of the out-of-towners and hop on a bus, or walk for 15 minutes, to the much smaller but more interesting Maltby Street Market. Here, you can drink gin cocktails (even in the morning), watch wholesalers prepping their products (hot sauce, smoked fish) and feast on the likes of steamed tamales, luxury waffles and just-baked sourdough flatbreads.

—

Borough Market, 8 Southwark Street, SE1 1TL.
(Full market open Wed to Sat).
020 7407 1002
www.boroughmarket.org.uk
London Bridge tube/rail.
Maltby Street Market, Ropewalk, SE1 2HQ.
(Open Sat and Sun).
www.maltby.st
Bermondsey tube or London Bridge tube/rail.

✦ KERB

One of the first high-quality street food collectives, KERB is also one of the most prolific. Its biggest showing (Tuesday to Friday lunchtimes) is at newly gentrified King's Cross, on a pristine square with plenty of seating at scattered bistro tables or on a large set of steps carpeted in astroturf alongside Regent's Canal. There are also various appearances at Spitalfields, the Gherkin, Paddington and the UCLU campus, plus the KERB Clubhouse in Hackney Wick. The rotation of handpicked traders is always excellent and usually offers a mix of meat (artisan burgers, meatballs, salt beef), spice (curried rotis, fashionable Korean tacos), and something sweet (doughnut bites, experimental brownies).

—

Granary Square (main summer location), N1C.

www.kerbfood.com

King's Cross St Pancras tube/rail.

FINEST INGREDIENTS.

- ALL OF OUR PACKAGING i

+ FULLY COMPOSTABLE

(JUST ASK IF YOU WANT US TO

AWAY FOR YOU)

HAPPY. EATING

AT THE DI

BRITISH STREET

✦ MARKET ROW & BRIXTON VILLAGE

Markets are great, aren't they? Except when the weather's cold and wet. This is where Brixton's two main 'arcades' (Market Row and Brixton Village) come into their own. Unlike unpredictable open-air street food stalls, these daily covered markets provide clusters of permanent little eateries where you can dine day or night, sitting outside but under cover among the record shops, fishmongers and Afro-Latino supermarkets. Though you can play it safe at pioneers-turned-chains like Honest Burger (Brixton Village) and Franco Manca (sourdough pizza, Market Row), it's worth exploring the more eclectic offerings of Brixton Village. Look out for French & Grace's Middle Eastern wraps, Okan's Japanese omelettes and Mama Lan's handmade Chinese dumplings. And if the sun's out, head for the three alfresco seating areas by the Coldharbour Lane/Atlantic Row entrance, one of which adjoins excellent Thai café KaoSarn.

—

Market Row, SW9 8LD and Brixton Village Market, Coldharbour Lane, SW9 8PR.
www.brixtonmarket.net/brixton-village
Brixton tube/rail.

✦ NETIL MARKET & BROADWAY MARKET

The simplest way to reach these markets is by bike or bus, which means the gawping tourist count is nicely low. For hot eats, especially on a Saturday, when there are stalls in addition to the permanent units, start at the tiny walled Netil Market or in the playground of London Fields Primary School – it's an extension of Broadway Market, and you can buy vintage vinyl plus the likes of lobster dumplings, fish tacos, venison hot dogs or shrimp brioche burgers there. Then wander past the popular Cat & Mutton pub and on to Broadway Market itself. Here, there's more hot food, plus stalls of the good-for-a-posh-picnic variety: luxury scotch eggs, artisanal breads, exotic cheese and olives, all with the sounds of a busker or two. Finish at the canal, with a stroll along the towpath.

Netil Market, Westgate Street, E8 3RN and Broadway Market, E8 4QJ.
www.netilmarket.com
www.broadwaymarket.co.uk
London Fields rail.

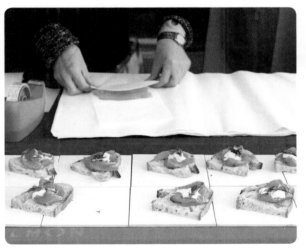

LATE NIGHT

Hungry Londoners

24 HOURS A DAY
7 DAYS A WEEK

THERE'S NO TIME TO BE TIRED

Come & Enjoy

★ ★ ★ ★ ★

WE USE RED TRACTOR ASSURED
⇐ & 100% BRITISH MEAT ⇒

LATE NIGHT

Last orders 11pm or later on a Saturday night

We're a city of night owls who love to dine out after hours. And that doesn't mean eating a dodgy kebab on the back of the night bus, or queuing up at Brick Lane Beigel Bake – the salt beef bagels are amazing, but you can forget about resting your bottom. We mean a proper sit-down-in-town dinner. If it's just a midnight eggs benedict on a Saturday you're after, there are two iconic old-timers: Vingt Quatre in Chelsea (or its slightly soulless sister branch off Tottenham Court Road) and Balans on Old Compton Street, which is ancient, but still great for Soho people-watching. This selection digs a bit deeper to uncover the most interesting places to extend your late night.

✦ DIRTY BONES

Picture an edgy Shoreditch bar-diner dropped on to a posh Kensington street and you've pretty much got Dirty Bones. On arrival, the hostess will greet you, not at a desk, but a pinball machine. You can't book ahead, but don't worry: the bar is as much of a draw as the restaurant with well-mixed cocktails and DJs spinning tunes. Once you're in the retro-ritzy dining room, you'll spot the mix of herringbone wooden floors, funky tiles and vintage record players – a lot of money has gone into making this place look old-school cool. As for the eats, they're 'gourmet diner' – that's posh hot dogs, 'bones' (barbecue ribs and some of the best fried chicken in town) and ditch-the-diet sides (mac 'n' cheese, chilli fries).

20 Kensington Church Street, W8 4EP.
020 7920 6434
www.dirty-bones.com
Kensington High Street tube.

✦ DUCK & WAFFLE

For a late-night bite that'll knock your socks off, nothing tops Duck & Waffle. Not only do you get *that* glass-sided express lift ride to the top – which also carries diners up to Sushisamba (p131) – but you can party in the bar before heading to the buzzy dining room for breathtaking London vistas. Cooking is luxurious and rich, from crunchy curls of barbecue-spiced pigs' ears to the signature dish: a waffle topped with a crisp-skinned, slow-cooked duck leg and a fried duck egg, served with a jug of mustard maple syrup. Bookend that with the likes of roasted octopus and chorizo, and a decadent dark chocolate brownie sundae, and you won't go to bed hungry.

—

40th Floor, Heron Tower, 110 Bishopsgate, EC2N 4AY.
020 3640 7310
www.duckandwaffle.com
Liverpool Street tube/rail.

✦ HIXTER BANKSIDE

A short stroll from Borough Market (p67), this Mark Hix steak and chicken restaurant is hugely popular with groups of local workers, and it's easy to see why. There's a big, bustling main dining room with a large open kitchen, a more intimate anteroom, and a cocktail bar downstairs. The 'cock 'n' bull' menu is fairly priced, too. The whole chook is a must-try – it comes upright and with its talons still on, and it's only £25 but able to feed three; the steak is costlier but still good value. Just don't skip the small stuff: the salads (shaved raw cauliflower with creamy Berkswell and hazelnuts), sides (proper fries, 'salt and vinegar' onion rings) and puds (vanilla ice cream with honeycomb and hot pouring chocolate) are worth making space for.

—

16 Great Guildford Street, SE1 0HS.

020 7921 9508

www.hixterbankside.co.uk

Borough tube or London Bridge tube/rail.

BRANCHES: Hixter City, City EC2M 4AE; Tramshed, Shoreditch EC2A 3LX.

SIBLINGS: Hix (Mayfair W1S 4BP; Soho W1F 9UP); Hix Oyster & Chop House, Barbican EC1M 6BN.

✦ POLO 24

You guessed it: this Bishopsgate stalwart is open 24 hours a day. Polo has been going since 1953, but it has reinvented itself as many times as Madonna and looks every bit the modern retro diner. On the ground floor, it's full of gleaming white brick tiles, school chairs and booths; for something cosier, head upstairs, where retro metal signs hang on exposed brick walls and seats are studded leather. The food is mostly Rule Britannia, with a bit of the Star Spangled Banner thrown in. There's bubble and squeak, welsh rarebit and sausage and mash, as well as pancakes, burgers and milkshakes. Thanks to its 24-hour booze licence, you can even upgrade your full fry-up to a 'Royal' version with added bubbles.

—

176 Bishopsgate, EC2M 4NQ.
020 7283 4889
www.polo24hourbar.co.uk
Liverpool Street tube/rail.

SEE ALSO (By last orders on Saturdays):

- Brilliant: 11pm (p151)
- Bob Bob Ricard: 11pm (p97)
- Dozo: 11pm (p168)
- Foxlow: 11pm (p92)
- Palomar: 11pm (p45)
- Polpo: 11pm (p23)
- Ceviche: 11.15pm (p39)
- Roka: 11.15pm (p24)
- Hawksmoor: 11.15pm, later in the bar (p156)
- Nobu: 11.20pm (p170)
- Babaji: 11.30pm (p54)
- Balthazar: 11.30pm (p13)
- Flesh & Buns: 11.30pm (p90)
- Princi: 11.30pm (p62)
- Tayyabs: 11.30pm (p151)
- Viet Grill: 11.30pm (p152)
- Berners Tavern: 11.45pm (supper menu only; p143)
- Brasserie Zédel: 11.45pm (p89)
- J Sheekey Oyster Bar: 11.45pm (p100)
- La Bodega Negra: 11.45pm (p144)
- Dishoom: 11.50pm (p108)
- Bone Daddies: midnight (p56)
- Dean Street Townhouse: midnight (p17)
- Herman ze German: midnight (p59)
- Ranoush Juice: midnight (p150)
- Smoking Goat: midnight (p46)
- Hakkasan: 12.15am (p99)
- Meatliquor: 12.30am (p157)
- Sushisamba: 12.30am (p131)
- Spuntino: 12.45am (p47)
- Lahore Kebab House: 1am (p151)
- Maroush I: 1am (p150)
- Pizza East: 1am (p93)

SPECIAL OCCASIONS

GROUP BIRTHDAYS

DATE NIGHTS

SPECIAL OCCASIONS
GROUP BIRTHDAYS AND DATE NIGHTS

You might think picking a restaurant for a big group would be easy
in London, but it comes with its own set of challenges. Not only do
you have to co-ordinate diaries with multiple people living on multiple
tube lines, but you also have to find somewhere good enough to silence
the complainers who will call you out on anything, from an annoying
location to poor music. Here's a selection of places that are not only
fun and easy to reach, but that actually have at least one decently
sized table designed for eight.

And from the mighty to the intimate... of all the eating-out occasions,
date night is the trickiest to negotiate. Do you go high-end and swanky?
Keep it casual? Look no further than this pick of failsafe spots to get that
relationship fizzing. What they all have in common is a terrific ambiance,
so if it turns out you have nothing to say to each other, it'll hopefully be a
little while before you notice.

GROUP BIRTHDAYS

✦ BRASSERIE ZÉDEL

So you like the razzmatazz grand-café vibe of
The Wolseley, but you're not a high roller? Then
consider this: Brasserie Zédel is The Wolseley's
affordable cousin, delivered by the same crack
team and sharing many of its glamorous features,
including a boisterous Art Deco room with marble,
brass rails and glittering chandeliers. The key
difference is its more workaday Gallic menu (steak
frites, salmon with dijon creamed leeks, deep-fried
whiting with tartare sauce), but this, together with
an approachable, egalitarian vibe, and the fact
that it has two large round tables seating up to
ten each, makes it a great place for groups. Don't
forget to stop for a Sazerac or two at the classy,
sleekly retro Bar Américain across the hall.

----

20 Sherwood Street, W1F 7ED.
020 7734 4888
www.brasseriezedel.com
Piccadilly Circus tube.
SIBLINGS: Colbert, Chelsea SW1W 8AX; Fischer's,
Marylebone W1U 5HN (p98); The Wolseley, Mayfair
W1J 9EB.

✦ FLESH & BUNS

The buns in the name of this Covent Garden basement joint are the steamed hirata variety, originally a Taiwanese street food, but adopted and made famous by cult NYC ramen bars Momofuku and Ippudo. You stuff them with cooked meat or fish, then add greens, pickles and sauces. At Flesh & Buns, from the same crew as ramen bar Bone Daddies (p56), the sharing portions of fillings include baby chicken with citrus-chilli rub and crispy piglet belly with a mustard miso glaze.

There are small plates too (prawn tempura rolls, Korean chicken wings), so bring lots of friends and arrive hungry.

—

41 Earlham Street, WC2H 9LX.
020 7632 9500
www.fleshandbuns.com
Covent Garden tube.
SIBLINGS: Bone Daddies (Kensington Wholefoods W8 5SE; Soho W1F 0AR).

✦ FOXLOW

For Hawksmoor founders Will Beckett and Huw Gott to describe their Clerkenwell baby as a 'neighbourhood restaurant' is to undersell its appeal. A winning combo of warm, clubby space (complete with cocktail bar) and terrific service, it's great for groups. Its upstairs gallery has three U-shaped leather booths which seat seven, and it's here you can share out the likes of curried mussels, smokehouse rillettes, ten-hour beef shortrib with kimchi and of course top-drawer steaks. But do save room for a calorific pud, such as the Elvis Presley ice cream sandwich: worth bursting out of your onesie for.

69-73 St John Street, EC1M 4AN.
020 7014 8070
www.foxlow.co.uk
Farringdon tube/rail.
BRANCHES: Stoke Newington N16 0AS.

✦ PIZZA EAST

Poor old pizza. Rather than being thought of as 'destination' food, it all too often gets munched on the street or in soulless chains. But Pizza East is a place to get your Oyster card out for. It now stands at three sites – all loud and stylish – but this original branch is a particularly worthy place to visit. The sexed-up Italian-American small plates (lamb meatballs, baked shin of veal bone marrow) are a draw in themselves, but wait till you try the pizza. Topped with the likes of finocchiona (Tuscan fennel salami) and robiola (soft mixed-milk cheese), they'll ensure you never order a four seasons again.

———

56 Shoreditch High Street, E1 6JJ.
020 7729 1888
www.pizzaeast.com
Shoreditch High Street Overground.
BRANCHES: Kentish Town NW5 1TL;
Portobello W10 5TA.

✦ PIZZA PILGRIMS

These days, good times in Soho don't necessarily have to be of the pornographic variety. Gastronomic good times abound, not least at Pizza Pilgrims. What began as a market stall with a near-evangelical following, serving one calzone and two 'bianca' (white base) options, now has two branches in the area – the slightly cramped Dean Street original, or this more spacious Kingly Court setting. The outside tables, much like those at Shoryu (p137) are great for affordable alfresco, but the inside is where to take your gang.

Downstairs, you'll not only find a giant Super Mario Bros mural, but two 'under-arch' booths, each seating eight and ideal for birthdays, and a large communal table for 10 to 12. The only downside? You have to arrive super-early, as you can't book.

—

11 Kingly Court, W1B 5PW.
020 7287 2200
www.pizzapilgrims.co.uk
Oxford Circus or Piccadilly Circus tube.
BRANCHES: Soho W1D 3PR.

More dedicated tables for 8-plus that you can book in advance:

- Balthazar, p13 – four round tables for 8.
- Begging Bowl, p13 – one bench table for 8-10.
- Berners Tavern, p143 – six booths for 7-8; one long table for 8-12.
- Bocca di Lupo, p36 – one table for 8; one table for 10.
- Boundary Rooftop, p127 – one table for 8.
- Brilliant, p151 – two round tables for 8.
- Bull & Last, p116 – one table for 8.
- Burger & Lobster, p14 – two booths for 8-9, one table for 10-12.
- Caravan, p107 – one (otherwise communal) table for 14.
- Chiltern Firehouse, p15 – two tables for 8.
- Colbeh, p150 – one square table for 12.
- Copita, p164 – two (otherwise communal) tables for 10-12.
- Dean Street Townhouse, p17 – three booths for 8-9.
- Dishoom, p108 – one table for 8-9
- Dozo, p168 – one square table for 8.
- Ember Yard, p165 – one 'high' table for 8.
- Grain Store, p18 – one 'high' table for 12, one table for 14.
- Hawksmoor, p156 – one table for 8.
- Hixter Bankside, p81 – one oval table for 8.
- Joy King Lau, p172 – several tables for 8, 10 or 12.
- Lahore Kebab House, p151 – two tables for 8.
- Maroush I, p150 – two round tables for 8-9.
- Min Jiang, p128 – three tables for 8, one table for 10, one table for 12 (all round).
- Nobu, p170 – four round tables for 8-12.
- Phoenix Palace, p174 – several tables for 8, 10 or 12.
- Princess Victoria, p120 – one round table for 8.
- Riding House Café, p113 – one (otherwise communal) table for 20.
- Roka, p24 – two tables for 8
- Royal China, p174 – several tables for 8, 10 or 12.
- The Shed, p25 – butcher's table for 12-13.
- Shoryu, p137 – two tables for 8-10.
- Smokehouse, p138 – one almond-shaped table for 8.
- Tayyabs, p151 – two tables for 8.
- The Camberwell Arms, p118 – two tables for 8, to tables for 10.
- Viet Grill, p152 – two tables for 8.
- Wright Brothers, p48 – one table for 8.

DATE NIGHTS

✦ BOB BOB RICARD

'Welcome to the dining car, madam. You may place your hat above your compartment and dim the lights here.' They don't actually say this when you arrive at Bob Bob Ricard, but they could. Deliciously eccentric, it's styled to look like the first-class dining car of an Edwardian train, with sumptuous Art Deco booths, a dress code ('elegant') and even a button to call for champagne. The reliably good food is Anglo-American grill meets Tsarist Russia (waldorf salad or caviar plus lobster mac 'n' cheese, smoked borscht and beef wellington). For a glitzy late-night option in central London, Bob Bob is more than a faux means of transport: it's a destination. Ladies and gents... all aboard!

—

1 Upper James Street, W1F 9DF.
020 3145 1000
www.bobbobricard.com
Piccadilly Circus tube.

✦ FISCHER'S

Oozing old-school romance, Fischer's is an ideal place to forget about the outside world. It may be from the same team as The Wolseley and Brasserie Zédel (p89), but while its relatives are high ceilinged, light and loud, Fischer's is low lit, warm and intimate – no matter how brightly the sun is shining outside. Modelled on a turn-of-the-century Viennese konditorei (patisserie), it's exceptionally good at the sweet stuff: fruit tarts, slices of decadent sachertorte (dark chocolate and apricot cake), three kinds of strudel. But before you get to that, there's smoked fish, posh sausages, with sauerkraut, *natürlich*, plus the must-have schnitzel. Fischer's does plenty of standard European dishes too (poached halibut, steak), but why order those, when you can canoodle over sweet knödel?

—

50 Marylebone High Street, W1U 5HN.
020 7466 5501
www.fischers.co.uk
Baker St tube.
SIBLINGS: Brasserie Zédel, Soho W1F 7ED (p89); Colbert, Chelsea SW1W 8AX; The Wolseley, Mayfair W1J 9EB.

✦ HAKKASAN

Dimming the lights isn't always a prerequisite for romance, but it's not a bad start. At this swanky subterranean Cantonese restaurant, the whole place is cloaked in near-darkness, from the sleek ebony room dividers with Oriental-style latticework, to the ultra-low setting of the lighting. Only the individual bulbs dangling over each table (so that you can actually see what you're eating) would make any kind of dent on the electricity bill. The Michelin-starred cooking is superb – as you'd expect at these tooth-sucking prices – lending finesse to high-street dishes (jasmine tea-smoked pork ribs, sesame prawns on toast) and smarter options (the signature roasted silver cod with champagne, for example). A seriously sexy spot.

—

8 Hanway Place, W1T 1HD.
020 7927 7000
www.hakkasan.com
Tottenham Court Road tube.
BRANCHES: Mayfair W1J 6QB.
SIBLINGS: HKK, Moorgate EC2A 2BE.

✦ J SHEEKEY OYSTER BAR

You know what they say — oysters are the ultimate aphrodisiac. But even if the slippery little bivalves aren't your thing, this younger sibling of the celebrated J Sheekey restaurant — open until midnight most nights — can't fail to get you in the mood. It oozes all the old-world glamour of next door, but with less formality. The seating is mostly around a gorgeous U-shaped marble counter, on comfy bar stools with backs, plus there are cosy tables next to the silvered, no-pry windows. The warm, low lighting makes supermodels of us all, the seafood-centred menu (gleaming shellfish; the signature fish pie; the squid and scallop burger) is terrific, and the wine list features plenty of champagne. And that's definitely an aphrodisiac.

—

33-34 St Martin's Court, WC2N 4AL.
020 7240 2565
www.j-sheekey.co.uk
Leicester Square tube.
SIBLINGS: Balthazar, Covent Garden WC2B 5HZ (p13); Bam-Bou, Fitzrovia W1T 1DB; The Ivy Market Grill, Covent Garden WC2E 8PS; J Sheekey, Covent Garden WC2N 4AL; Scott's, Mayfair W1K 2HE.

SEE ALSO:

SOMETHING FOR THE WEEKEND

BREAKFAST & BRUNCH

SUNDAY ROAST

SOMETHING FOR THE WEEKEND
BREAKFAST, BRUNCH & ROAST

When it comes to kicking off the weekend after a big Friday
night, Londoners love a full-on full English breakfast accompanied
by a builder's brew (extra-strong, sugary tea), or a hair-of-the-dog
Bloody Mary to help the hangover. If it's socialising not recovery that's
in order, we tend to follow Manhattan's lead by using late-morning brunch
to catch up with friends in a place that looks as good as the food tastes.
For the last classic weekend meal – the Sunday roast – expectations are
always high. The setting needs to be cosy, the atmosphere needs
to be warm and the kitchen needs to be dishing up only the finest meat
and trimmings. This chapter features top places that definitely cut the
mustard. Or horseradish. Or mint sauce.

BREAKFAST & BRUNCH

✦ ALBION

Don't be fooled by the east London postcode or the trad name: this is not some workers' caff. Actually, it's the light, airy ground-floor space of the Boundary building, which houses a fashionable café, restaurant, bar and rooftop restaurant (p127) created by veteran designer Terence Conran. Iconic red Tolix chairs line the front alfresco strip, as does vibrant produce in wooden crates and wicker baskets. Head in (via a gourmet deli, of course) and you'll find a modern rustic room with long wooden tables and industrial lighting. Happily, this is not a case of style over substance: the British food is beautifully cooked, whether it's game pie, roast chicken or a glorious full English from the all-day menu. There's also duck eggs on toast, a breakfast bap and a calorie-controlled sweet potato hash if you're there early.

—

2-4 Boundary Street, E2 7DD.
020 7729 1051
www.albioncaff.co.uk
Shoreditch High Street Overground.
BRANCHES: South Bank SE1 9FU.

✦ CARAVAN

If it's Kiwi cooking you're after, Caravan is king. Larger than the Exmouth Market original, this King's Cross flagship is housed in an old grain warehouse (shared with Grain Store, p18), giving the place a sexy, bare-brick, Manhattan loft vibe. There's an on-site coffee roaster, airy indoor seating and a patch of outdoor tables looking out across Granary Square. From the ever-evolving all-day menu, you'll find bold global flavours (deep-fried duck egg with baba ganoush; mackerel fillet with seaweed), while pizza toppings are no less interesting (white anchovy with fennel and mascarpone). But the menu really shines at brunch with delights such as coconut bread with poached rhubarb or corn and morcilla fritters. Just be patient: weekends brunch tables are no-bookings.

Granary Building, 1 Granary Square, N1C 4AA.
020 7101 7661
www.caravankingscross.co.uk
King's Cross St Pancras tube/rail.
BRANCHES: Exmouth Market EC1R 4QD.

✦ DISHOOM

It's impossible not to love this fashionable 'old Bombay' Irani-style café. Unlike the sometimes touristy Covent Garden original, the Shoreditch branch feels more local. Despite its size, each section manages to feel warm and buzzy, thanks largely to its good looks: dark patterned tiles, exposed girders, vintage lighting, distressed walls and – in the large conservatory – a leafy, colonial-style 'verandah'. The affordable all-day menu offers the likes of black daal, grilled masala prawns or spiced lamb chops. But it's especially brilliant in the mornings, when you can tuck into bacon naan rolls, eggs on chilli cheese toast or the with-a-kick Big Bombay, with Ginger Pig bacon and masala beans.

—

7 Boundary Street, E2 7JE.
020 7420 9324
www.dishoom.com
Shoreditch High Street Overground.
BRANCHES: Covent Garden WC2H 9FB;
King's Cross N1C 4AB.

✦ E PELLICCI

Fed up with froufrou fry-ups? You know the kind
– sourdough toast, heritage tomatoes and eggs
from hens with names? Then you need E Pellicci.
This iconic East End caff, open until 4pm daily, has
been going strong since 1900 and knocks out old-
fashioned, back-to-basics full English breakfasts for
an appreciative crowd of locals and food tourists.
Portions are huge and typically include fried eggs,
a puddle of baked beans, juicy sausage, fatty bacon,
fried tomatoes, fried mushrooms, bubble
and squeak and black pudding. All served up in
Grade-II listed surrounds by members of the
jovial Pellicci family. You can also tuck into pies,
fish and chips, or plates of Italian home cooking.
Timewarp-tastic.

—

332 Bethnal Green Rd, E2 0AG.
020 7739 4873
No website
Bethnal Green tube/rail.

✦ FOX & ANCHOR

A handsome, lovingly refurbished Victorian boozer, Fox & Anchor has glorious panelled wooden snugs, vintage tiling and swirly wallpaper. To match its interior, it also dishes up classy pub grub (oysters, devilled chicken livers, wild boar and apple bangers). At brekkie, this Clerkenwell favourite comes into its own, serving Bloody Marys, Bucks Fizz and Bellinis alongside smoked haddock fritters, sausage and egg baps, or welsh rarebit with eggs. As for fry-ups, there's a classic Full Monty, but if you're feeling really bullish, take on a City Boy: a pimped-up version which includes a minute steak, lamb kidney, calves' liver, fried bread and a pint of stout.

—

115 Charterhouse Street, EC1M 6AA.
020 7250 1300
www.foxandanchor.com
Barbican tube or Farringdon tube/rail.

✦ MODERN PANTRY

For a bright, bold, Antipodean brunch full of fusion flavours, you could go to Marylebone's still-excellent, always bustling Providores, where the movement first began. For those flavours in a uniquely tranquil setting, make for Modern Pantry, which is run by Canadian-born, Kiwi-raised chef Anna Hansen (one of the co-founders of Providores). Inside, the place is long and lean, clinical and clean; outside, it's a different story. A paved, traffic-free suntrap, it's a lovely space to enjoy raspberry and ricotta pancakes, halloumi with slow-roast tomatoes, or the signature sugar-cured prawn omelette with smoked chilli sambal. Can't get up in time for brunch? It's a great setting for the reimagined afternoon tea, too.

—

47-48 St John's Square, EC1V 4JJ.
020 7553 9210
www.themodernpantry.co.uk
Farringdon tube/rail.

112

✦ RIDING HOUSE CAFÉ

You know those US TV shows where everyone lives in Manhattan in improbably large apartments and goes to brunch in stylish, sexy restaurants full of young trendies? Well, walking into the Riding House Café is like walking on set – in a good way. There's sleek wood, there's leather, there are gleaming tiles. Even the loos are gorgeous. Though it's strong on small plates, the weekend brunch menu stays full-sized with a mix of classics (buttermilk pancakes, reuben sarnies) and with-a-twist dishes (lobster eggs benedict, or the New Orleans eggs hussarde, made with rich red wine and bone-marrow bordelaise). Plus several salads, for those of you who really want to eat like an Emmy-winning TV star.

—

43-51 Great Titchfield Street, W1W 7PQ.
020 7927 0840
www.ridinghousecafe.co.uk
Oxford Circus tube.

✦ SUNDAY

The name says it all. This little neighbourhood hangout is a place that considers Sundays special. And at the centre of it all? Brunch. The menu changes constantly, but expect the likes of toasted banana bread, buttermilk pancakes with honeycomb butter, blueberries, bacon and maple syrup, corn fritters with kiln-smoked salmon, avocado, tomato and crème fraîche, or welsh rarebit with smoked haddock, bacon and a poached egg. It's even more adventurous in the evenings when the changing menu offers the likes of labneh-stuffed piquillo peppers, seared scallops with corn arancini and chorizo, or damson and soured cream tart with mascarpone ice cream. And you don't have to wait for a month of Sundays — it's actually open every day except Monday.

—

169 Hemingford Road, N1 1DA.
020 7607 3868
No website
Caledonian Road & Barnsbury Overground.

SEE ALSO:

- Balthazar, p13
- Barnyard, p35
- Berners Tavern, p143
- Chiltern Firehouse, p15
- Dean Street Townhouse, p17
- Duck & Waffle, p79
- Fischer's, p98
- Foxlow, p92
- Grain Store, p18
- Honey & Co, p42 – Saturday only
- Lido Cafe, p132
- Ottolenghi, p180
- Polo 24, p82
- Princi, p62

SUNDAY ROAST

✦ BULL & LAST

Visit this Highgate institution at any time and you'll eat exceptionally well – it's one of a small breed of London pubs where the food is better than you'll find at most restaurants. Seasonal dishes change daily, from autumnal pappardelle with hare ragu, to a lamb schnitzel sarnie with frites and mint relish, followed by excellent homemade ices (millionaire, Ferrero Rocher, cherry sorbet). But to come on a Sunday, when you can first go for a bracing yomp across neighbouring Hampstead Heath, is truly special. The best of the week's à la carte is available, plus the likes of roast pork belly with roast potatoes, roast pears, black pud and crackling; or roast sirloin of beef with yorkshire puddings and picture-perfect trimmings.

—

168 Highgate Road, NW5 1QS.
020 7267 3641
www.thebullandlast.co.uk
Gospel Oak rail/Overground.

✦ THE CAMBERWELL ARMS

This spruced-up old south-east London boozer – from the same crew that gave us Waterloo's Anchor & Hope – excels itself on the day of rest. And unlike at the A&H, you might actually stand a chance of getting a table. There's more than just roasts, from pork fat and scotch bonnet on toast or curried parsnip soup with an onion bhaji, to rabbit and smoked bacon pie. The roast itself is often served for the table, whether it's pot-roast pheasant with buttered parsnips and mustard sauce for two; or slow-roast shoulder of lamb with dauphinoise potatoes and purple sprouting broccoli, for four. Sharing is caring, you know.

----

65 Camberwell Church Street, SE5 8TR.
020 7358 4364
www.thecamberwellarms.co.uk
Denmark Hill rail/Overground.
SIBLINGS: The Anchor & Hope, Waterloo SE1 8LP; The Canton Arms, Stockwell SW8 1XP; Great Queen Street, Covent Garden WC2B 5AA.

✦ LAMBERTS

There's nothing Joe Lambert doesn't know about beef. He's hugely passionate about his seasonal British produce, much of it from local farms, and his zeal comes through in the modern British cooking at this smart neighbourhood restaurant. There's an excellent monthly-changing à la carte (as well as great-value midweek set meals), but it's on Sundays that Lamberts excels. Enthusiastic staff dish up the likes of whole roasted partridge with game chips, old spot pork belly with crackling, or slices of classic rare roasted angus rump with yorkshire pud and all the trimmings. For the truly ravenous there are also classy British starters (salt-baked beetroot; oat-crusted herring) and puds (hedgerow trifle; Neal's Yard cheeses). Time to put some posh in your Sunday nosh.

———
2 Station Parade, Balham High Road, SW12 9AZ.
020 8675 2233
www.lambertsrestaurant.com
Balham tube/rail.

✦ PRINCESS VICTORIA

The gastropub was born in west London, and while there are arguably more famous examples (like the Cow in Westbourne Park), the cooking at this handsome, friendly neighbourhood spot takes some beating, especially when it comes to Sunday roast. The three options might run to tender, pink slices of Cumbrian beef rib with nicely chewy yorkshire puds, Dingley Dell pork belly with crackling and apple sauce, or roasted and spiced Cotswold chicken with tomato and chilli salsa.

All served with cooked-in-dripping tatties and colourful seasonal veg. Bar snacks (cured meats, scotch eggs, pickles), starters (pork and green peppercorn pâté, smoked fish) and puds (peanut fudge, goats' cheesecake with damson jelly) are equally brilliant — so put on your fat pants.

—

217 Uxbridge Road, W12 9DH.
020 8749 5886
www.princessvictoria.co.uk
Shepherd's Bush tube/rail/Overground.

SEE ALSO:

- Barnyard, p35
- Berners Tavern, p143
- Dean Street Townhouse, p17
- Fox & Anchor, p111
- Foxlow, p92
- Harwood Arms, p20
- Hawksmoor, p156
- Pizza East, p93
- Smokehouse, p138

SENSATIONAL SETTINGS

SENSATIONAL SETTINGS

It is a truth universally acknowledged that a restaurant with a fantastic setting will often become lazy and rest on its good-looking laurels. Happily, there are a handful of places across town that offer the full package: lovely things to look at, great food and excellent service. And here they all are. First up are Rooms With A View – dining rooms that, when you're not looking at your food, are all about looking out of the window. Then there's the Alfresco selection: spaces where it's a delight to sit outside (rather than being crammed by the side of a smoggy road). And finally, the Rooms To Remember selection… these are the 'wow factor' dining rooms so spectacular your jaw drops when you walk in – or, the theme is so convincing it's like entering a parallel universe.

ROOMS WITH A VIEW

✦ BOUNDARY ROOFTOP

Living in tightly packed London, it's hard not to be a sucker for a rooftop. But the sense of space you get from this crowning glory of Terence Conran's Boundary project (also home to a basement restaurant and Albion, p106) would make even a welly-wearing country type swoon. A study in contemporary chic, it combines huge olive trees and stylish garden tables with glass, steel and even an outdoor fireplace. If it rains, don't worry: you can dine under a glass canopy trailed with climbers. The summery grill menu offers simple delights, properly executed: from shellfish platters and oysters to tuna and fennel salad, steak and whole lobster with fries. Order a glass of fizz and watch the sun go down on the City.

—

2-4 Boundary Street, E2 7DD.
020 7729 1051
www.theboundary.co.uk
Old Street tube/rail or Shoreditch High Street Overground.

✦ MIN JIANG

They should have called this Cantonese hotel restaurant 'Duck with a View'. The signature Beijing duck, though expensive, justifies the 45-minute wait (tip: order it in advance of arriving). It comes three ways: carved at your table to go in pancakes; skin-only, for dipping into fine sugar; and cooked into one of four dishes, such as stir-fried with rice. There's also terrific dim sum and seafood, and even the noodles are excellent, as well as being a good way to keep the bill from rocketing. The dining room may be tasteful rather than thrilling, but if you're not ogling the food, you'll be gazing out of the windows, at peaceful views stretching across Hyde Park.

—

10th Floor, Royal Garden Hotel, 2-24 Kensington High Street, W8 4PT.
020 7361 1988
www.minjiang.co.uk
High Street Kensington tube.

✦ SUSHISAMBA

Calling all glamourpusses: this is the cat's meow. Start with an exhilarating ride up the glass-sided lift to the 38th floor (worth the trip alone), go for cocktails on one of the two terraces (or the indoor bar if it's cold), then head into the large, open-plan dining room where wraparound glass means that wherever you sit you'll get spectacular skyline views. The food, as the name suggests, is a fusion of Japanese and Latin flavours, such as crispy taquitos with yellowtail, avocado and roasted corn miso; scallop ceviche with pickled mandarin and shiso; or a twist on miso black cod, here cooked as an anticucho (a skewer, from the robata grill). It's quite genius.

—

Floors 38 & 39, Heron Tower, 110 Bishopsgate, EC2N 4AY.
020 3640 7330
www.sushisamba.com
Liverpool Street tube/rail.

SEE ALSO:
- Duck & Waffle, p79

ALFRESCO

✦ LIDO CAFE

This is no ordinary public pool caff. First off, the 50-metre lido is a glittering shade of azure: more Hockney than Herne Hill. The café's outdoor seating extends the holiday vibe, with giant cream umbrellas and potted palms. Inside, it's industrial-chic high ceilings, concrete floor and funky wallpaper. The cooking is simple, yet special: black pudding on sourdough for brunch; mackerel bap with homemade tartare sauce for lunch; wild rabbit with wild mushrooms and grilled polenta for dinner. The only annoyances are the queue and the occasionally frantic service, so book ahead (it's open daily from 9am until 11pm every day except Sunday and Monday, when it closes at 5.30pm). And remember to allow time for a stroll around the glorious Brockwell Park afterwards.

—

Brockwell Lido, Dulwich Road (Herne Hill end), SE24 0PA.
020 7737 8183
www.thelidocafe.co.uk
Herne Hill rail.

✦ PETERSHAM NURSERIES CAFÉ

This daytime-only restaurant (there's a teahouse too), is preposterously idyllic – you can sit either outside around a fountain shaded by foliage, or under a glass roof draped with bamboo mats (which make it look and feel like an exotic canopy). There are climbers and shrubs, dressers of pot plants and colonial-style furnishings (wooden ceiling fans, photos from the Raj). The floor is packed-down soil, so you might see the odd bug, but this all adds to the charm. Exquisite plates of modern European food, using produce from the garden whenever possible, complete the picture. This boho experience comes at a hefty price, but it's definitely one for your (garden) bucket list.

—

Petersham Nurseries, Church Lane, off
Petersham Road, Richmond, TW10 7AB.
020 8940 5230
www.petershamnurseries.com
Richmond tube/rail.

✦ SHORYU

There are several branches of this excellent ramen bar, including ShoryuGo, the only one to offer takeaway, but the one in Kingly Court is the best. Why? Well first of all, you can enjoy Shoryu's range of top-quality Japanese comfort food (including eight kinds of Tonkotsu ramen, plus gyoza dumplings, hirata buns and the like) in the semi-alfresco surroundings you'd normally pay a sizeable premium for. It's a smart, enclosed courtyard, shared with other restaurants, including Pizza Pilgrims (p94). But even if you're not outside, the light indoor space feels marvellously 'zen'. Unlike its siblings, you can book ahead – though the outside spots remain first-come, first-served.

—

3 Kingly Court, London, W1B 5PJ.
No phone
www.shoryuramen.com
Oxford Circus tube.
BRANCHES: Mayfair SW1Y 4LR; Soho W1D 7HA; and Shoryu Go, Soho W1B 5AG.

✦ SMOKEHOUSE

The term 'hidden gem' gets bandied around a lot, but in the case of this tucked-away Islington spot, it's bang-on. Shielded from traffic by dark foliage, the 50-seat outdoor space has a magical, secret-garden vibe to it, with elegant furniture and twinkly fairy lights. Cooking is highly creative smokehouse-with-a-twist: perhaps a deep-fried oyster with beef dripping toast and smoked bone marrow, ahead of smoked duck with kimchi and potato cake. For more formal alfresco, sit on the slim dining terrace down the side of the building, but do watch the weather forecast, as there are no heaters or parasols. Still, as consolation prizes go, the relaxed, pubby interior will do nicely.

—

63-69 Canonbury Road, N1 2DG.
020 7354 1144
www.smokehouseislington.co.uk
Highbury & Islington tube/rail/Overground.
BRANCHES: Chiswick W4 4LD.

✦ TOWPATH

Longing for a simpler life? Then wander over to this canalside spot where there's no phone, no website and no wi-fi. And no, you can't book. To help you out, you should know it opens Thursdays to Sundays from 9am until dusk plus 9am–5pm on Tuesdays and Wednesdays, but only from the first Tuesday in March until early November – they like to close with the fireworks. Most of the tables are on the towpath itself, under a retractable awning. The only inside bit is the shallow lock-up, which holds two long skinny tables, so expect to get cosy. Everything is homemade, from the unassuming breakfasts to the peanut butter in the cookies. Turn up at lunch and you'll really see Towpath shine, with its daily-changing seasonal menu billing the likes of globe artichoke with lemon butter, or roast chicken with borlotti beans, pumpkin and aioli.

—

Regent's Canal towpath, between Whitmore Bridge and Kingsland Road Bridge, N1 5SB.
No phone, no website
Haggerston Overground.

SEE ALSO:
- Boundary Rooftop, p127
- Caravan, p107
- Chiltern Firehouse, p15
- Grain Store, p18
- Modern Pantry, p112
- Pizza Pilgrims, p94
- Tonkotsu, p64

ROOMS TO REMEMBER

✦ BERNERS TAVERN

If you want to worship at the Temple of Atherton (that's chef Jason Atherton, darling of London's dining scene), you may prefer his Mayfair restaurants, including fine-dining flagship Pollen Street Social, or its more accessible Brit-leaning brother Social Eating House (p26). But this offshoot in Fitzrovia's terribly cool Edition Hotel has something they don't: a truly unique dining room. High-ceilinged, with grand lighting and gilded picture frames, it practically gushes with glamour. In among the high-end grill dishes, Atherton groupies will find more inventive offerings, such as mac 'n' cheese with braised ox cheek and bone marrow crumble; or ham hock and a poached, breaded egg set over pea and bean risotto, playfully dubbed 'ham, egg and peas'.

—

The London Edition Hotel, 10 Berners Street, W1T 3NP.
020 7908 7979
www.bernerstavern.com
Oxford Circus or Tottenham Court Road tube.
SIBLINGS: City Social, Moorgate EC2N 1HQ; Little Social, Mayfair W1S 1NE; Pollen Street Social, Mayfair W1S 1NQ; Social Eating House, Soho W1F 7NR (p26).

✦ LA BODEGA NEGRA

Seedy DVDs not your thing? Don't feel like a lapdance today? Never fear, the neon signs at 9 Old Compton Street are all just part of its tongue-in-cheek disguise. Venture inside to be greeted by a PVC-clad mannequin gimp, plus a glamorous real human to take your coat. Head downstairs, wait for your eyes to adjust (it's as dark as a nightclub), and into the large, subterranean space, more 'sexy cave' than basement. Split into buzzy cocktail bar and trendy restaurant, La Bodega Negra has an electric atmosphere and charming staff to boot. The Mexican food (from tiny tacos and tostaditas to the more substantial grilled meats) is perfectly good, but you don't go for the food. You go to hang out in the best sex shop in town.

—

9 Old Compton Street, W1D 5JE.
020 7758 4100
www.labodeganegra.com
Leicester Square tube.
SIBLINGS: La Bodega Negra Cafe, Soho W1D 5NH.

✦ L MANZE

To make like a proper old Cockney, you have to have a plate of pie and mash. And if you happen to be near this iconic spot, you'll get a fair whack of history thrown in for free. Open since 1929, it's the longest continuously open pie-and-mash shop in the capital, with original interiors (dark wood booths, shimmering wall tiles, embossed ceiling) so gobsmackingly gorgeous that English Heritage awarded them a Grade-II listing. Don't go expecting a gourmet experience: the mash often gets slopped off a spoon school-dinner-style and the green parsley gravy, also known as 'liquor', can be offputting to the uninitiated. But the pies themselves, served until 4pm early in the week (or 5pm Thursday to Saturday) are a puffy-topped slice of old London life.

—

76 High Street, E17 7LD.
020 8520 2855
No website
Walthamstow Central tube/rail.

SEE ALSO:
- Barnyard, p35
- Bob Bob Ricard, p97
- Chiltern Firehouse, p15
- Dishoom, p108
- Fischer's, p98
- Fox & Anchor, p111
- Hakkasan, p99
- J Sheekey Oyster Bar, p100
- Meatliquor, p157

AROUND THE WORLD

AROUND THE WORLD

It's a cliché, but so true: London is an enormous melting pot.
At last count, the city could boast more than 70 different world cuisines
within Zones 1 to 6. And Londoners know where to find the authentic
flavours of another land, heading to South Kensington for the best
French food, New Malden for Korean, Ealing for Polish, Green Lanes for
Turkish, Stockwell for Portuguese… There isn't room to cover all of these
in detail, so this chapter covers the three cuisines most enduringly popular:
Middle Eastern, South Asian and Vietnamese. Following that, there's a
roll-call of destination restaurants that will satisfy a craving for a particular
dish, from dim sum to steak and tapas. So don't bother with that pricey
plane ticket… just grab your Oyster card.

MIDDLE EASTERN

For a taste of the Middle East without leaving the capital, go for a walk down Edgware Road. The stretch between Marble Arch and Edgware Road tube stations will transport you to a more exotic place, with its vibrant grocery stores and shisha smokers sat outside street cafés. Traditional stalwarts include the various Maroush branches specialising in Lebanese cooking: for a sit-down meal, go to **Maroush I** (pictured), which stays open till 2am and has belly-dancing from 9.30pm. For a more casual bite, queue for **Maroush Express**, or even spin-off street food and juice specialist **Ranoush Juice**, where the shawarma wraps are delicious and cheap. If it's fragrant Persian stews, freshly baked flatbreads and mouthwatering grills you're after, head down the side streets into the likes of **Patogh**, with its cramped, rough-plastered, straight-off-the-streets-of-Tehran vibe, friendly staff and great-value cooking. Or try smarter Connaught Village alternative **Colbeh**, which has a colourful tiled floor, a beautiful clay oven in the window and pretty fabric-covered tables, plus a large table for 12 under the skylight at the back. Of course, because Levantine food (dishes from southern Turkey to northern Egypt via Syria, Lebanon and Israel) has become high fashion, you can now find modern options such as Palomar (p45) or Honey & Co (p42) in other parts of town.

—

- Maroush I, 21 Edgware Rd, W2 2JE. Marble Arch tube.
- Maroush Express, 68 Edgware Rd, W2 2EG. Marble Arch tube.
- Ranoush Juice, 43 Edgware Rd, W2 2JE. Marble Arch tube.
- Patogh, 8 Crawford Place, W1H 5NE. Edgware Road tube.
- Colbeh, 6 Porchester Place, W2 2BS. Edgware Road tube.

SOUTH ASIAN

Savvy diners know there's no such thing as generically 'going for an Indian'. The best Subcontinental restaurants in London tend to showcase the cooking of a distinct South Asian region: some within India (Gujarat, Kerala), some spanning borders (the Punjab) and some neighbouring (Bangladesh, Pakistan, Sri Lanka). To get a flavour of south Asian sub-culture, from the gold jewellery dealers to the glittering fabrics of the sari shops, start in Wembley. Here, you'll find great examples of Gujarati vegetarian cuisine, particularly at **Sakoni's**. South of the river in Tooting, it's a case of authentic Sri Lankan and South Indian at **Apollo Banana Leaf** and café-plus-dining-room **Jaffna House**. For Indian Punjabi curries and grills, go west to Southall and visit the **New Asian Tandoori Centre** and the brilliant **Brilliant**. Alternatively, set yourself on a course to Whitechapel in the east for excellent Pakistani Punjab at cult favourite **Tayyabs** (pictured). Challengers to Tayyabs' throne include the nearby **Needoo Grill** and **Lahore Kebab House**. As for Brick Lane around the corner... just give it a miss.

- Sakoni's, 127-129 Ealing Rd, HA0 4BP. Alperton tube.
- Apollo Banana Leaf, 190 Tooting High St, SW17 0SF. Tooting Broadway tube.
- Jaffna House, 90 Tooting High St, SW17 0RN. Tooting Broadway tube.
- New Asian Tandoori Centre, 114-118 The Green, UB2 4BQ. Southall rail.
- Brilliant, 72-76 Western Rd, UB2 5DZ. Southall rail.
- Tayyabs, 83-89 Fieldgate St, E1 1JU. Aldgate East tube.
- Needoo Grill, 87 New Rd, E1 1HH. Aldgate East tube.
- Lahore Kebab House, 2 Umberston St, E1 1PY. Aldgate East tube.

VIETNAMESE

Unlike many of London's other culinary hubs, Kingsland Road does not pair its regional (Vietnamese) cuisine with country-specific shops. As in, it is not a microcosm of Hanoi: there are no street hawkers or motorbike repair shops here. Still, it's not known as Pho Mile for nothing (pho being the rice noodle soup that Vietnam calls its national dish). On a short stretch of road, you'll find well over a dozen restaurants to suit every occasion. If you're on a budget and don't mind being rushed in and out of a packed, garish-green, canteen-style dining room, book ahead – or expect to queue – for **Sông Qûe Café**. Here, the papaya salad, summer rolls and pho are all terrific. For a more tranquil experience (though the room is a tad higgledy-piggledy), seek out friendly **Mien Tay**, which specialises in dishes from the south-western region of Vietnam. Try the stir-fried goat with galangal and the whole crispy fried sea bream with fish sauce and mango. If you're after something more smart and special, then go for **Viet Grill**, where the good-looking room is matched by handsome dishes such as cooked-at-the-table 'la vong' grilled monkfish, or a clay pot of delicious braised, simmering catfish. Round off with a Vietnamese coffee.

—

- Sông Qûe Café, 134 Kingsland Rd, E2 8DY. Hoxton Overground.
- Mien Tay, 122 Kingsland Rd, E2 8DP. Hoxton Overground.
- Viet Grill, 58 Kingsland Rd, E2 8DP. Hoxton Overground.

STEAK & DUDE FOOD

✦ FLAT IRON

Meat lesson for beginners: 'flat iron' is a butcher's term which actually comes from the US. It's a relatively inexpensive but full-flavoured cut of beef that in the right hands can become a thing of beauty. Which is exactly what this trendy Soho joint does. Having begun life as a pop-up and pub residency, it finally went bricks 'n' mortar in 2012 with this miniature steak house (it has a handful of shared tables, plus a few downstairs). Apart from the odd special, all it serves is flat iron steak. But bloody marvellous — and marvellously bloody — it is: charred on the outside, pink and juicy in the middle. Decent cocktails add to the hip vibe.

—

17 Beak Street, W1F 9RW.
No phone
www.flatironsteak.co.uk
Piccadilly Circus or Oxford Circus tube.
BRANCHES: Covent Garden WC2H 8LS.

✦ HAWKSMOOR

Hawksmoor is the benchmark that all steakhouses should be measured against. The quality and cooking of the British meat (up to eight cuts change daily, and are chalked on a blackboard) is exceptional. But where Hawksmoor really stands a cut above the competition in its relaxed, accessible attitude. Too many steakhouses take themselves seriously, preaching to weary customers about meat-hanging techniques and so on. The warm, friendly staff here will only show off their impressive knowledge if you actually want them to. There are now several branches of Hawksmoor, but this subterranean Covent Garden dining room remains one of the buzziest, partly thanks to its excellent destination bar (where the award-winning Bloody Marys are superb).

—

11 Langley Street, WC2H 9JG.
020 7420 9390
www.thehawksmoor.co.uk
Covent Garden tube.
BRANCHES: Bank EC2V 5BQ; Knightsbridge SW3 2AL; Mayfair W1J 0AD; Spitalfields E1 6BJ.

✦ MEATLIQUOR

The burgers here are so irresistible that you not only have to queue to get in, you need to negotiate a militant doorman first. And god help you if one of your group is running late. The beefy bouncer patrols the long line, stamping hands – and if someone isn't there yet and misses their stamp... well, tough. You all have to go to the back – or, of course, abandon them. Then again, smiley waitresses pop out to hand out free snacks (deep-fried pickles; billowing onion rings), so perhaps it's not so bad to wait. Inside, it's more nightclub than restaurant: deafeningly loud music, graffiti on the walls, signs reading 'No suits, no ballet pumps'. Tattooed staff dish out artisanal burgers, terrific fries and cool cocktails. Friends still not arrived? Definitely time to ditch them.

---

74 Welbeck Street, W1G 0BA.

020 7224 4239

www.meatliquor.com

Bond Street tube.

BRANCHES: Angel N1 1QP.

SIBLINGS: Chickenliquor, Brixton SW9 8PR;
Meatmarket, Covent Garden WC2E 8BE;
Meat Mission, Hoxton N1 6HG.

✦ PATTY & BUN

Hats off to the crew at P&B for earning their stripes the hard way. Long before they opened this tiny West End spot (there's a newer sister branch in the City), they were flipping burgers at pop-ups, constantly taking on feedback and working harder to create the most magnificent burgers in town. And they've got it bang-on. Top-notch beef patties, plus lamb, buttermilk chicken and veggie options, are cooked medium rare and snuggled into soft brioche buns with secret weapons from the P&B arsenal including melted Red Leicester cheese and the outstanding housemade smoky mayo. Battered retro interiors and incredibly cool (but incredibly friendly) staff complete the package. Worth the queue.

—

54 James Street, W1U 1HE.
020 7487 3188
www.pattyandbun.co.uk
Bond Street tube.
SIBLINGS: Liverpool Street EC2M 7PD.

✦ PITT CUE CO

Before you visit this cult Soho joint, ask yourself the following questions: do you mind queuing? And are you claustrophobic? If it's no to both, you'll be fine. Having started out as a South Bank food cart, Pitt Cue put down permanent roots at this tiny site in 2012 and hasn't looked back since. Go early, or off-peak, or prepare to wait. Next, request a basement table, or expect to be jostled in the ground-floor bar. Finally, relax and tuck into some of the best barbecue cooking outside the Deep South. Smoky, tender ribs; melt-in-the-mouth pulled pork; creamy, calorific bone-marrow mash; and crunchy, zingy slaws – you'll go up a belt size, but it's well worth it.

—

1 Newburgh Street, W1F 7RB.
020 7287 5578
www.pittcue.co.uk
Oxford Circus tube.

SEE ALSO:

TAPAS

✦ BARRAFINA

The folks at this smart tapas bar have perfected the art of keeping the queue happy: they feed you while you wait. Yes, once you're over the threshold, you'll shuffle along the wall counter like a slow-moving line at the Ikea canteen, while supping on sherry and munching nibbles (toasted almonds, padrón peppers, ham croquetas). Just don't fill up too much: the real thrills come once you get your seat at the L-shaped counter. The chefs work at lightning speed to rustle up some of the finest classic tapas in town, including cured meat and tender grilled octopus, as well as soft, pillowy tortillas and charred, milk-fed lamb. Even the salads — such as baby gems with anchovies, pancetta and shallot dressing — are knockout.

—

54 Frith Street, W1D 4SL.
020 7813 8010
www.barrafina.co.uk
Leicester Square or Tottenham Court Road tube.
BRANCHES: Covent Garden WC2N 4HZ.
SIBLINGS: Fino, Fitzrovia W1T 1RR.

✦ COPITA

At first glance, this buzzy little room is the model of a traditional tapas restaurant. There's stool seating, plenty of good wine, a vibrant atmosphere and a changing menu of small plates. But don't come here expecting patatas bravas. Sure, you can always find a few classic offerings – cured meats, cheeses, gambas pil-pil prawns in chilli, garlic and oil – but it's Copita's creative flair that wows. Croquetas might be made with blue cheese; an escabeche (usually a pickled fish dish) with rabbit; and chips, actually more like thick crisps, tossed in paprika and topped with the runny yolk of a duck egg. Sit by the window for great people-watching.

—

26 D'Arblay Street, W1F 8EP.
020 7287 7797
www.copita.co.uk
Oxford Circus tube.
SIBLINGS: Copita del Mercado, Spitalfields E1 7AL.

✦ EMBER YARD

To fully understand this restaurant you have to go back to 2006. That's when Salt Yard, one of the first good small-plates restaurants, arrived on the capital's dining scene. Since then, other sister restaurants have opened: little Soho spot Dehesa; revamped Theatreland pub Opera Tavern and the largest of the four, Ember Yard. Warm, stylish, with great service and great wine, it takes the original Salt Yard formula of Spanish-meets-Italian-tapas and puts it over hot coals. The end result is smoky yet tender octopus with gutsy peperonata, sweet pepper and smoked ricotto arancini and Ibérico pork ribs with a quince glaze and celeriac puree. It's all stunning.

60-61 Berwick Street, W1F 8SU.

020 7439 8057

www.emberyard.co.uk

Oxford Circus or Tottenham Court Road tube.

SIBLINGS: Dehesa, Soho W1F 9BP; Opera Tavern, Covent Garden WC2B 5JS; Salt Yard, Fitzrovia W1T 4NA.

SEE ALSO:
- José, p43
- Morito, p44

SUSHI

✦ DININGS

If you love being in the know, then you'll love this stylish, low-key spot. Thanks to its unassuming location in a small townhouse on a quiet Marylebone backstreet, it rarely gets passing trade. A good thing too: without a reservation, you'll struggle to get in. This is partly because it's tiny, with just six seats at the ground-floor counter and 22 in the minimalist concrete-chic basement restaurant. But it's also because the sushi is sensational. Sweet, attentive staff serve the likes of tar-tar chips (crunchy potato tacos with fillings such as lobster, avocado and yuzu), steamed wagyu buns, blowtorched nigiri, and unimpeachable, gleaming sashimi. It's not cheap, but if you want contemporary sushi without all the Wags, it's perfect.

—

22 Harcourt Street, W1H 4HH.
020 7723 0666
www.dinings.co.uk
Marylebone tube/rail.

✦ DOZO

Dozo is a vampire. By day, it's sweet and gentle, by night it can have you bleeding from where it hurts: your wallet. It's perpetually stylish, in a Japanese spa kind of way, with a smart stone floor, plinky-plonky music and low lighting. There are several sunken tables giving the effect of sitting on the floor at a traditional low table, but without pulling a hamstring. The sushi is exceptional and service is polite, so if you are here for a smart dinner, you won't mind the bill. But the real steal is the set lunch: where else can you get a sashimi set with rice, salad, and miso of this quality, in this setting, for under a tenner?

—

32 Old Compton Street, W1D 4TP.
020 7434 3219
www.dozosushi.co.uk
Leicester Square or Tottenham Court Road tube.
BRANCHES: South Kensington, SW7 3LQ.

✦ KULU KULU

Sushi is expensive: it's labour-intensive to make and the raw ingredients are dear. You can often find decent lunch deals around, but if you want a sushi dinner that won't cost the earth try Kulu Kulu. This original branch on Brewer Street is a no-frills, student-friendly space offering all the fun of sitting at a kaiten (that's a conveyer belt, though there are a sprinkling of tables too), without a too-painful price tag. Try the made-to-order tempura prawn temaki (handrolls), which have been made here for two decades, the hot korroke (croquettes), plus cups of bottomless green tea. For an even more traditional vibe (but no conveyor), wander down to humble sister restaurant Ten Ten Tei at number 56.

---

76 Brewer Street, W1F 9TX
020 7734 7316
www.kulukulu.co.uk
Piccadilly Circus tube.
BRANCHES: Covent Garden WC2H 9JU;
South Kensington SW7 2HP.
SIBLINGS: Ten Ten Tei, Soho W1F 9TJ.

✦ NOBU

By rights, Nobu shouldn't be in this book. It's hideously expensive, the room is a dull '90s blonde and it's full of non-'real' Londoners: the oil-rich, Wags and celebrities. But if you are ever able to dine on someone else's pound, then this is the place to do it. Ever since Matsuhisa Nobu first brought his modish take on Nikkei (Japanese-Peruvian fusion) to the capital, the London sushi scene hasn't been the same. High rollers go for yellowtail sashimi with jalapeño, the 'new-style' sashimi and the celebrated black cod; better value (but equally delicious) are the tiger shrimp tempura and the anticucho (Peruvian-style) or kushiyaki (Japanese-style) meat skewers.

1st Floor, The Metropolitan, 19 Old Park Lane, W1K 1LB.
020 7447 4747
www.noburestaurants.com
Hyde Park Corner tube.
BRANCHES: Mayfair W1J 8DY.

✦ YASHIN SUSHI

'Without Soy Sauce' may be written on the awning outside this smart, buzzy Kensington sushi spot, but this enigmatic statement is not its name – it's the philosophy. Yashin aims to create modern sushi so perfectly composed – think seared eel with slivers of summer truffle and vinegar jelly, or tuna nigiri on crunchy rice with sea asparagus and garlic paste – that you simply won't need soy. You might want to reach for the matched sake though, which cutely comes in test tubes.

1a Argyll Road, W8 7DB.
020 7938 1536
www.yashinsushi.com
High Street Kensington tube.
SIBLINGS: Yashin Ocean House, South Kensington SW7 3RN.

SEE ALSO:
· Roka, p24

DIM SUM

◆ JOY KING LAU

Londoners understand that Chinatown, paradoxically, isn't the best place for dim sum. But if you are here on a DSM (Dim Sum Mission), then JKL is the place to be. Sure, it doesn't have the imperial decor and trolleys of some of the grander (but more touristy) Cantonese restaurants, or the slick styling of the Taiwanese teahouses, but it does do seriously good, affordable dim sum. The vibe can be hectic, mixing proper tablecloths with headset-sporting waitresses barking orders to the kitchen, so just focus on the food. There's a large selection with over eight kinds of cheung fun (filled rice noodles) and must-haves like the steamed pork, prawn and coriander dumplings.

---

3 Leicester Street, WC2H 7BL.

020 7437 1132

www.joykinglau.com

Leicester Square or Piccadilly Circus tube.

✦ PHOENIX PALACE

At first, Glenworth Street may look like just another dull route heading north off Marylebone Road, but this smart Cantonese restaurant at number 5 makes it a destination. By night, or if you order from the à la carte, it can be steep – you're paying for lavish ingredients and high-quality cooking. But for dim sum, especially given the standards and the glittering space, it's a real steal. Whether you're after classic steamed dumplings, cheung fun (giant stuffed rice 'cannelloni') and crispy spring rolls, or the more adventurous duck tongues with spicy sesame, or chicken claws in black bean sauce, it's all here. Just stick to the standard dim sum hours: noon to 5pm Monday to Saturday (and from 11am on Sundays). Now get thee to the Palace.

---

5 Glentworth Street, NW1 5PG.
020 7486 3515
www.phoenixpalace.co.uk
Baker Street tube.

✦ ROYAL CHINA

If you claim to like dim sum but haven't been to a Royal China, then you're not eating like a Londoner. There are a handful of branches across town, sporting the same winning formula: glossy black and gold oriental furnishings, well-drilled (if sometimes slightly scary) staff, a smart à la carte and one of the best 'yum cha' offerings in town. They're all bustling spaces, but this original branch is the most atmospheric and always has great people-watching opportunities, plus plenty of tables for big groups. The traditional dim sum menu, served noon to 5pm, sports all manner of Cantonese delights, from shimmering, translucent har gau (steamed prawn dumplings), to meat-centred glutinous rice parcels. You can book during the week, but expect to queue on weekends.

---

13 Queensway, W2 4QJ.
020 7221 2535
Bayswater or Queensway tube.
BRANCHES: Baker Street W1U 3BZ; Canary Wharf E14 8RR; Fulham SW6 5HE; and Royal China Club, Marylebone W1U 7AJ.

SEE ALSO:
- Hakkasan, p99
- Min Jiang, p128

SWEET STUFF

SWEET STUFF

The last ten years has seen a confectionery revolution in London. The city now has some of the world's finest pastry chefs, bakeries, ice-cream parlours and cake shops all serving top-notch sweet treats to a discerning clientele with refined taste. So if you're going to indulge in some chocolate, you'll find seriously decadent slabs made from the best cocoa; for pastry cravings, London has buttery, flaky examples as good as the ones in Paris. Same goes for ice cream – you can go for made-on-site gelato like the ones you've had in Rome. And as for cakes, let's just say we've come a long way from the Victoria sponge…

CAKES

At gorgeous bakery **Violet Cakes**, Californian-born Claire Ptak specialises in gold-standard US bakes, including buttercream-topped cupcakes (coconut milk, fragolina grape, salted caramel) that change with the seasons. For Scandinavian flavour, head down a dinky Covent Garden alley for even dinkier bakery **Bageriet** where you can sample Morotstårta (carrot cake) with lemon and vanilla cream-cheese icing, plus lesser-seen creations such as the Prinsesstårta (a traditional sponge cake with marzipan, raspberry jam, cream and custard). For a London classic, it has to be the irresistible vanilla-iced chocolate Curly Whirly cake at the original Waterloo bakery of **Konditor & Cook**. Or the equally iconic billowing pistachio and rosewater meringues, which always peer regally out of the window at the many branches of groundbreaking deli **Ottolenghi**.

—

- Violet Cakes, 47 Wilton Way, E8 3ED. Dalston Junction Overground.
- Bageriet, 24 Rose Street, WC2E 9EA. Leicester Square tube.
- Konditor & Cook, 22 Cornwall Road, SE1 8TW. Waterloo tube/rail.
- Ottolenghi, 21 Upper Street, N1 2TZ. Angel tube.

CHOCOLATE

So you're a card-carrying member of Chocoholics Anonymous? Well you're in the right place: London's top chocolatiers can kick the Continental bottoms of those in Brussels or Switzerland. Hotel Chocolat blazed an early trail, opening quality choc shops across the capital (some of which have seating), plus a devilishly inviting café called **Rabot 1745** in Borough Market. While over at artisan chocolatier **Paul A Young**, there is nothing that the staff can't do with salted caramel. Then there's the flagship Belgravia boutique of master pâtissier and chocolatier **William Curley**, which has seating both inside and out. Now throw away that Dairy Milk.

- Rabot 1745, 2 Bedale Street, SE1 9AL. London Bridge tube/rail.
- Paul A Young, 33 Camden Passage, N1 8EA. Angel tube.
- William Curley, 198 Ebury Street, SW1W 8UN. Sloane Square tube.

ICE CREAM & GELATO

Remember the dark days, when getting an ice cream meant some sad scoop of synthetic-tasting tutti frutti from a mobile vendor? Thank goodness they're over. Nowadays, London has heaps of high-quality dedicated gelaterias. Most, such as the excellent **Gelatorino**, deal in classic flavours. But others, such as Soho's **Gelupo**, are more inventive, with ever-changing concoctions such as ricotta, chocolate and black pepper or the hugely popular salted caramel and pecan. For something truly off-piste though, it has to be Camden's **Chin Chin Labs**. Here, in a mist of liquid nitrogen vapour, ice cream makers create brilliantly bizarre, weekly-changing flavours from chargrilled satsuma to dairy-free caramel crispy apple and sage.

—

- Gelatorino, 2 Russell Street, WC2B 5JD. Covent Garden tube.
- Gelupo, 7 Archer Street, W1D 7AU. Piccadilly Circus tube.
- Chin Chin Labs, 49-50 Camden Lock Place, NW1 8AF. Camden Town tube.

PASTRIES

For really old-school ooh-la-la, head to the bijou **Balthazar Boulangerie** in Covent Garden, into which the handsome Art Deco styling of the bustling main restaurant (p13) spills over. It's worth waiting for one of the little counter seats, so you can drink in the atmosphere while you feast on crumbly quiches, just-baked bread and exceptional pastries. There's a more futuristic vibe at South Kensington's candy-coloured **Pâtisserie des Rêves**. Here, the exquisite creations are kept under climate-controlled glass pods, and much of the seating is outdoors, café-culture-style. Still yearning for the Continent? Then pick up something from **Aux pain des Papys** (just minutes from the Eurostar terminal) and compare it with what's around the Gare du Nord in Paris. You'll see.

- Balthazar Boulangerie, 4-6 Russell Street, WC2B 5HZ. Covent Garden tube.
- Pâtisserie des Rêves, 13 Exhibition Road, SW7 2HE. South Kensington tube.
- Aux pain des Papys, 279 Gray's Inn Road, WC1X 8QF. King's Cross St Pancras tube/rail.

INDEX

VEGGIE-FRIENDLY

London is a great place to be a vegetarian. For every restaurant that leans on a dull dish (mushroom risotto, we're looking at you), there are plenty that, though they're not actually 'vegetarian' restaurants, will always have something interesting to offer a non-meat eater.

- Apollo Banana Leaf, p151
- Babaji, p54
- Begging Bowl, p13
- Bocca di Lupo, p36
- Caravan, p107
- Ceviche, p39
- Copita, p164
- Dishoom, p108
- Ember Yard, p165
- Grain Store, p18
- Hakkasan, p99
- Honey & Co, p42
- Hunan, p21
- Koya, p60
- Lyle's, p22
- Maroush I, p150
- Mien Tay, p152
- Min Jiang, p128
- Modern Pantry, p112
- Nobu, p170
- Phoenix Palace, p174
- Pizza East, p93
- Pizza Pilgrims, p94
- Polpo, p23
- Riding House Café, p113
- Royal China, p174
- Sakoni's, p151
- The Shed, p25
- Spuntino, p47
- Tayyabs, p151

LAST MINUTE

Changing your plans at the last minute (or simply not making any in the first place) is very London. So here's a list of the best places that you can get into at no notice. Most of them don't take bookings (though many do at lunch, or for large groups), so expect to queue.

- 10 Greek Street, p34
- Albion, p106
- Babaji, p54
- Barnyard, p35
- Barrafina, p162
- Begging Bowl, p13
- Bone Daddies, p56
- Boundary Rooftop, p127
- Burger & Lobster, p14
- The Camberwell Arms, p118
- Copita, p164
- Dishoom, p108
- Ducksoup, p40
- Flat Iron, p155
- José, p43
- Koya, p60
- Meatliquor, p157
- Morito, p44
- Patty & Bun, p158
- Pitt Cue Co, p160
- Pizza Pilgrims, p94
- Polpo, p23
- Princi, p62
- Shoryu, p137
- Smoking Goat, p46
- Spuntino, p47
- Tonkotsu, p64

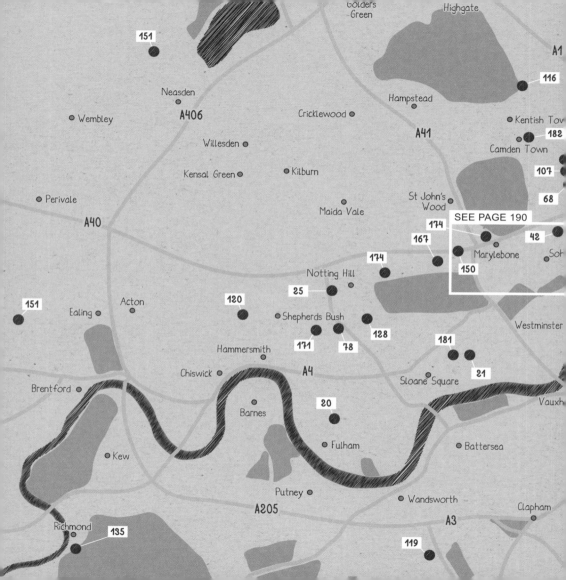

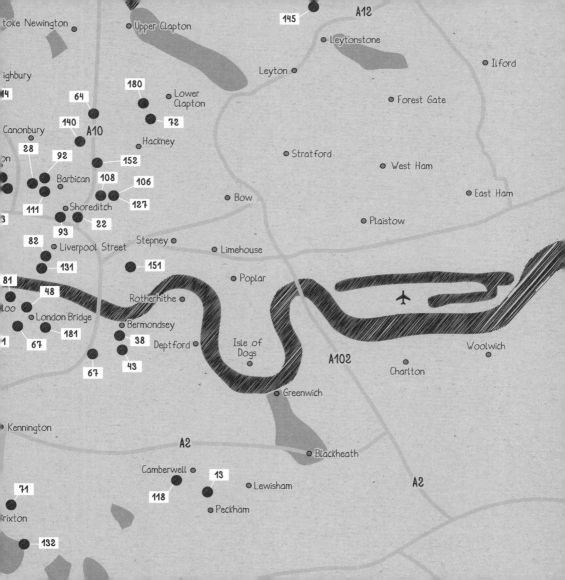

Frances Lincoln Limited
74–77 White Lion Street
London N1 9PF
www.franceslincoln.com

Eat Like a Londoner
Copyright © Frances Lincoln 2015
Text copyright © Tania Ballantine 2015
Photographs copyright © Kim Lightbody 2015
Except the following: p.106 Albion; p.127 Boundary
Rooftop; p.15 Chiltern Firehouse © Nicholas Kay; p.17
Dean Street Townhouse; p.111 Fox & Anchor; p.93
Pizza East; p.113 Riding House Café.
Design: Sarah Allberrey
Commissioning editor: Zena Alkayat

A catalogue record for this book is
available from the British Library.

ISBN 978-0-7112-3679-0
Printed and bound in China

9 8 7 6 5 4 3 2 1